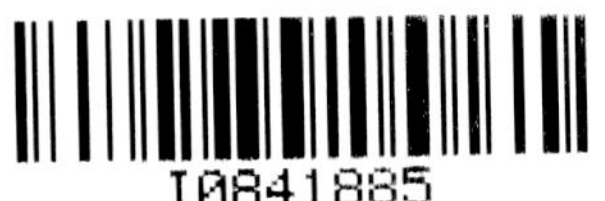

HOUSEPLANT
COLORING BOOK

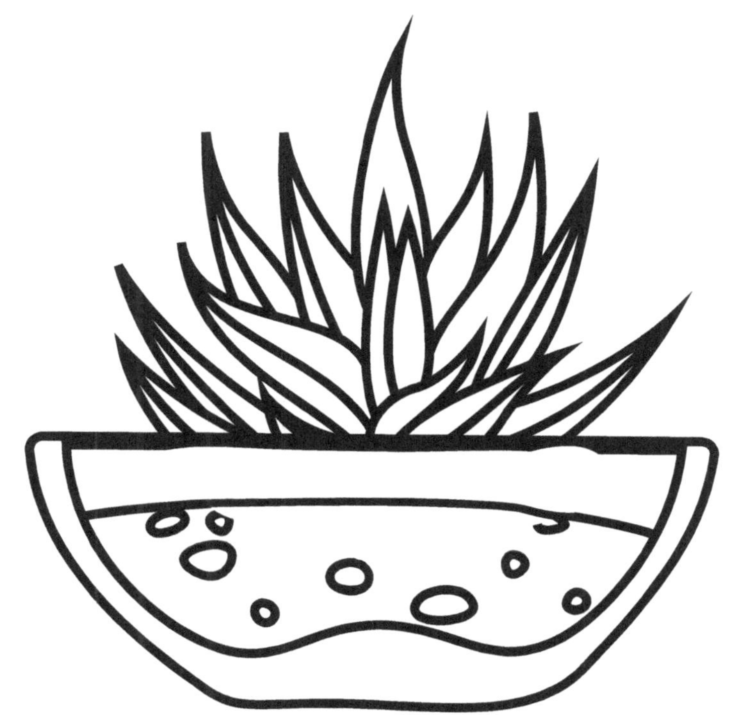

This Book Belongs to:

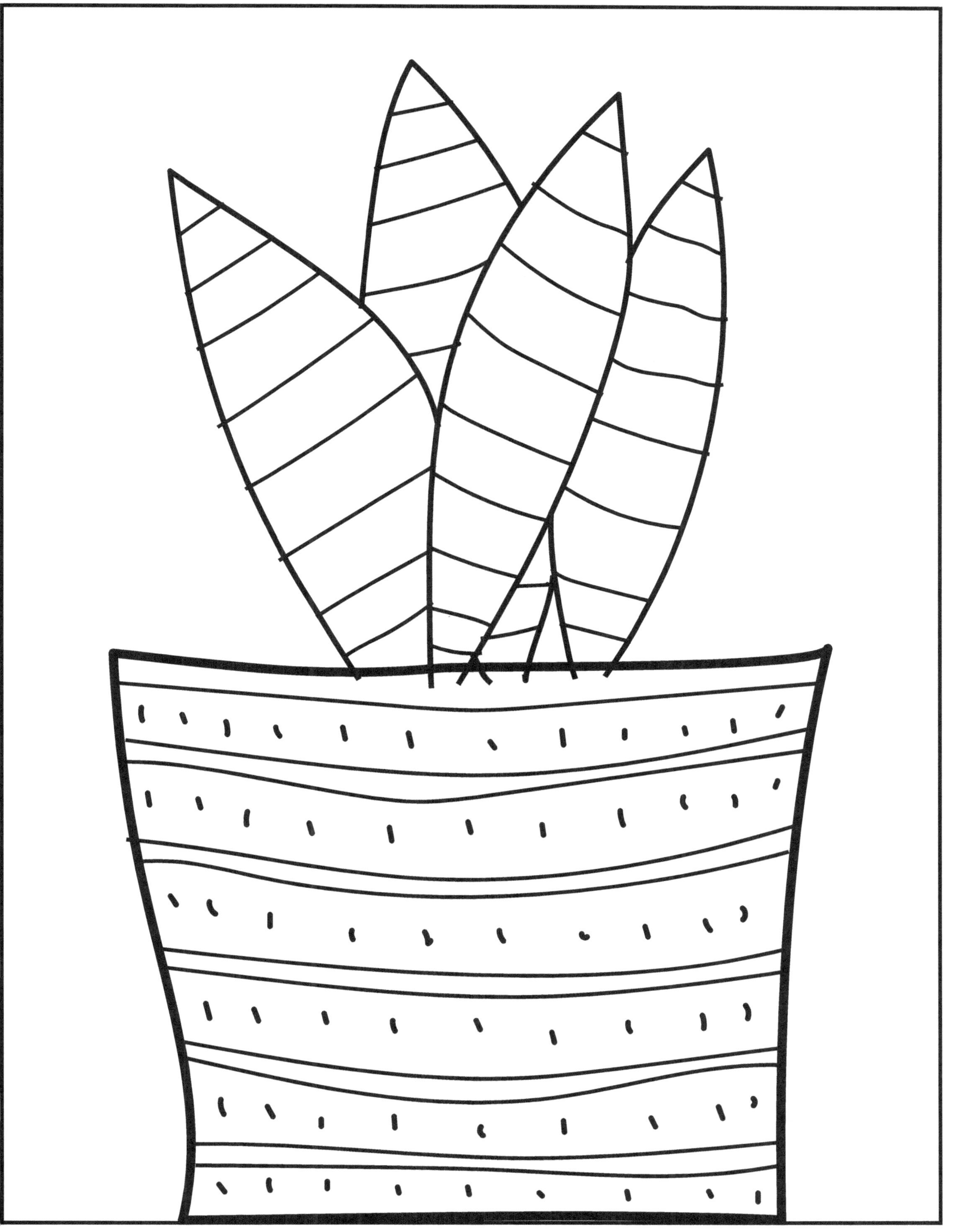

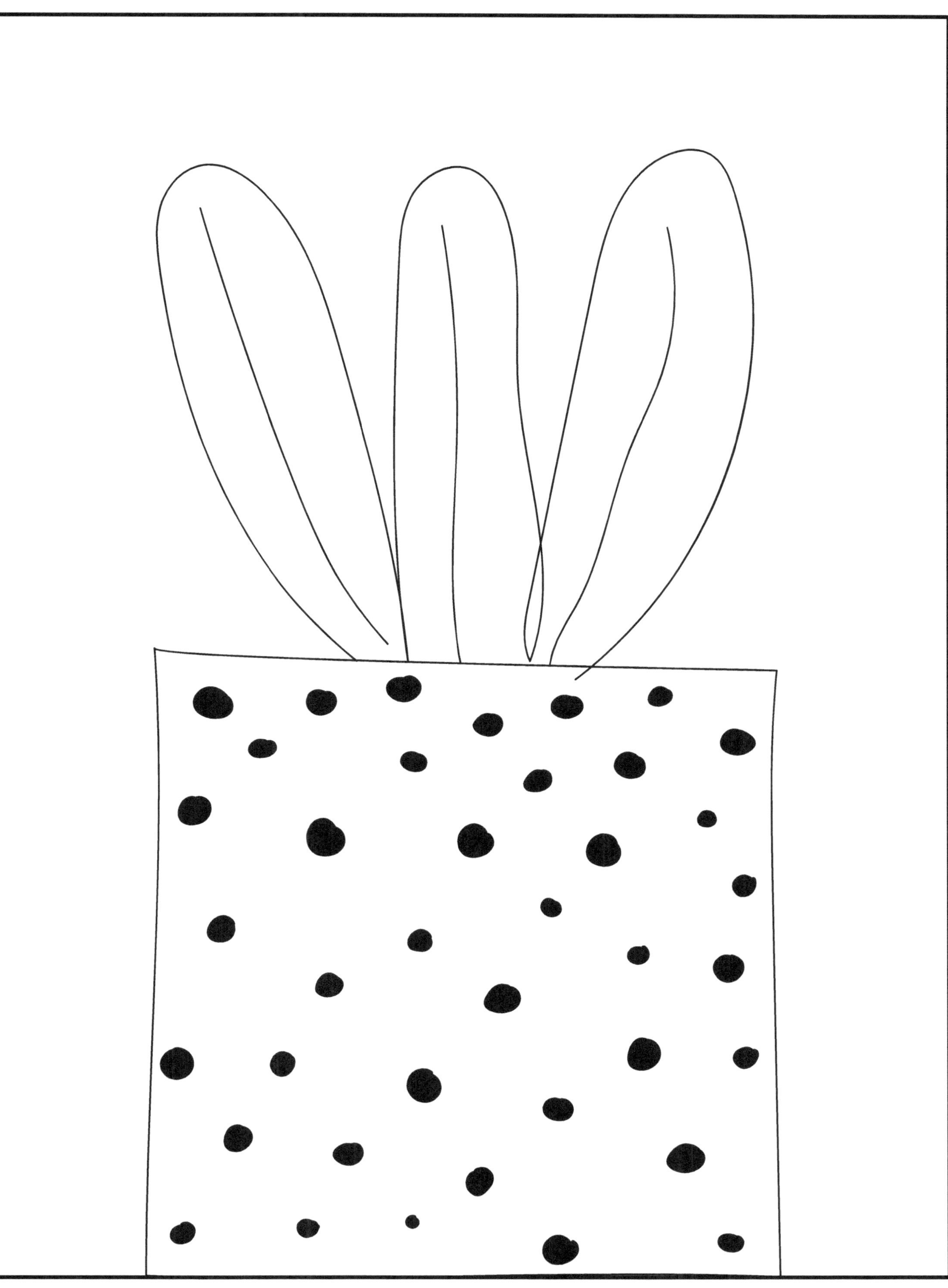

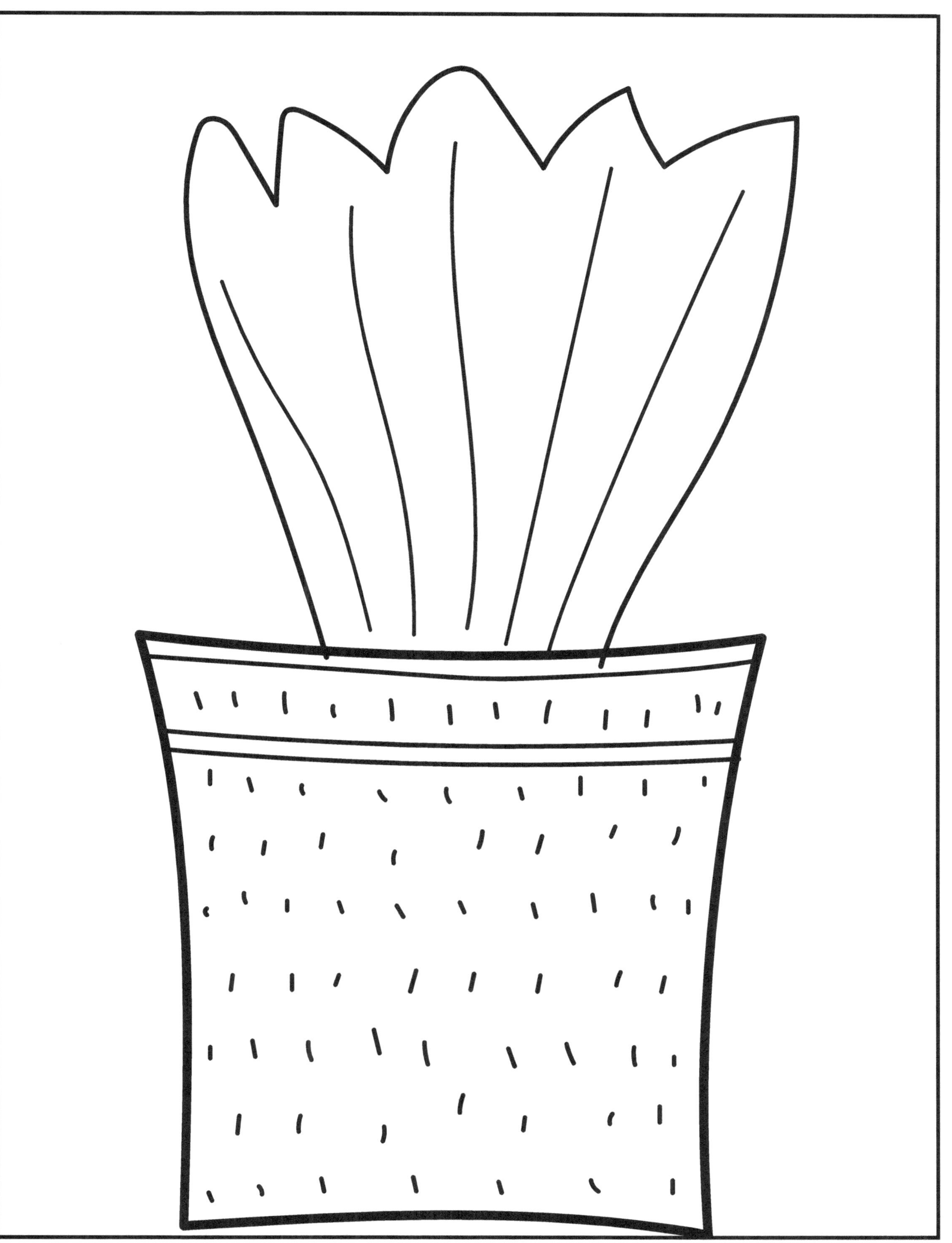

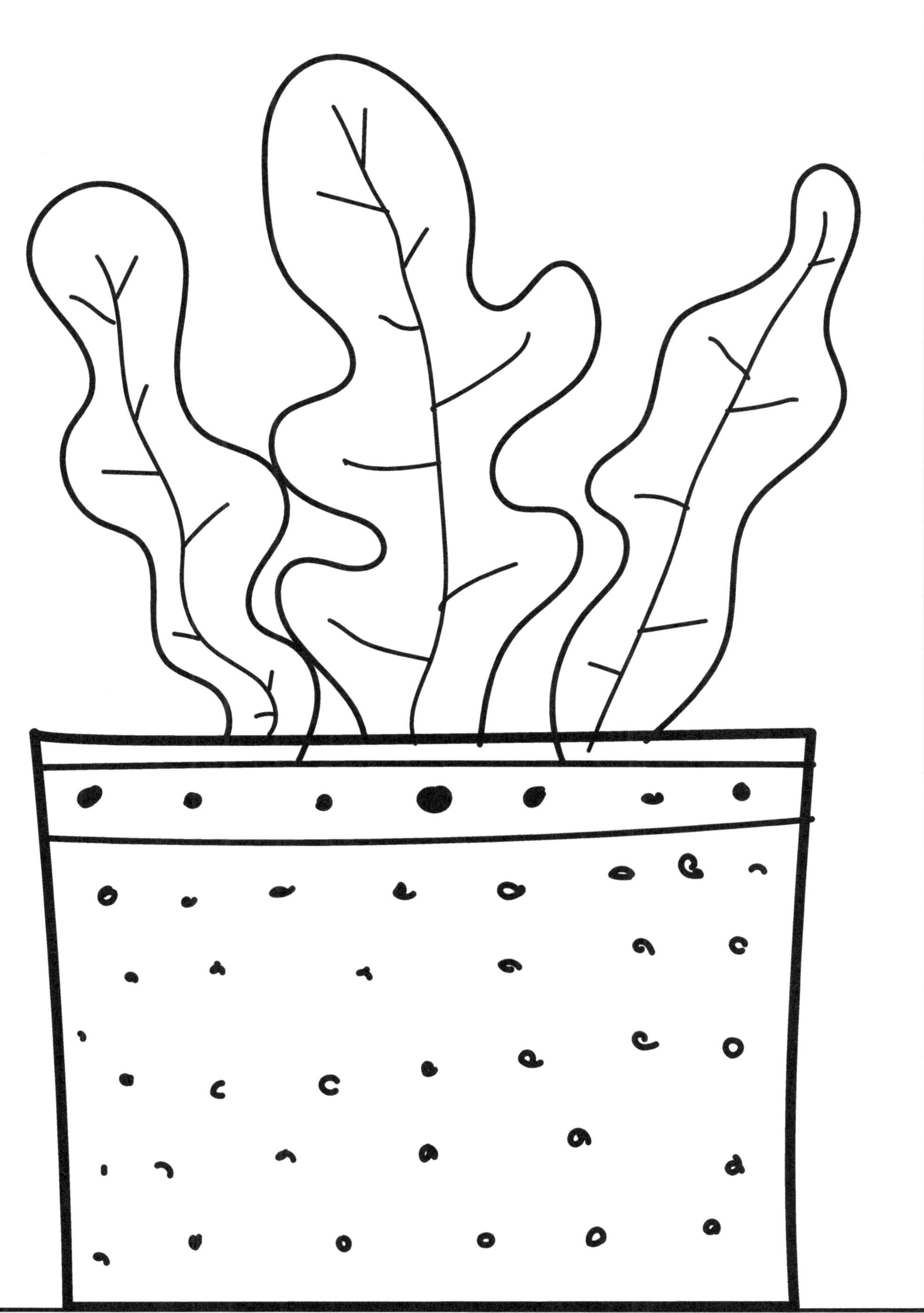

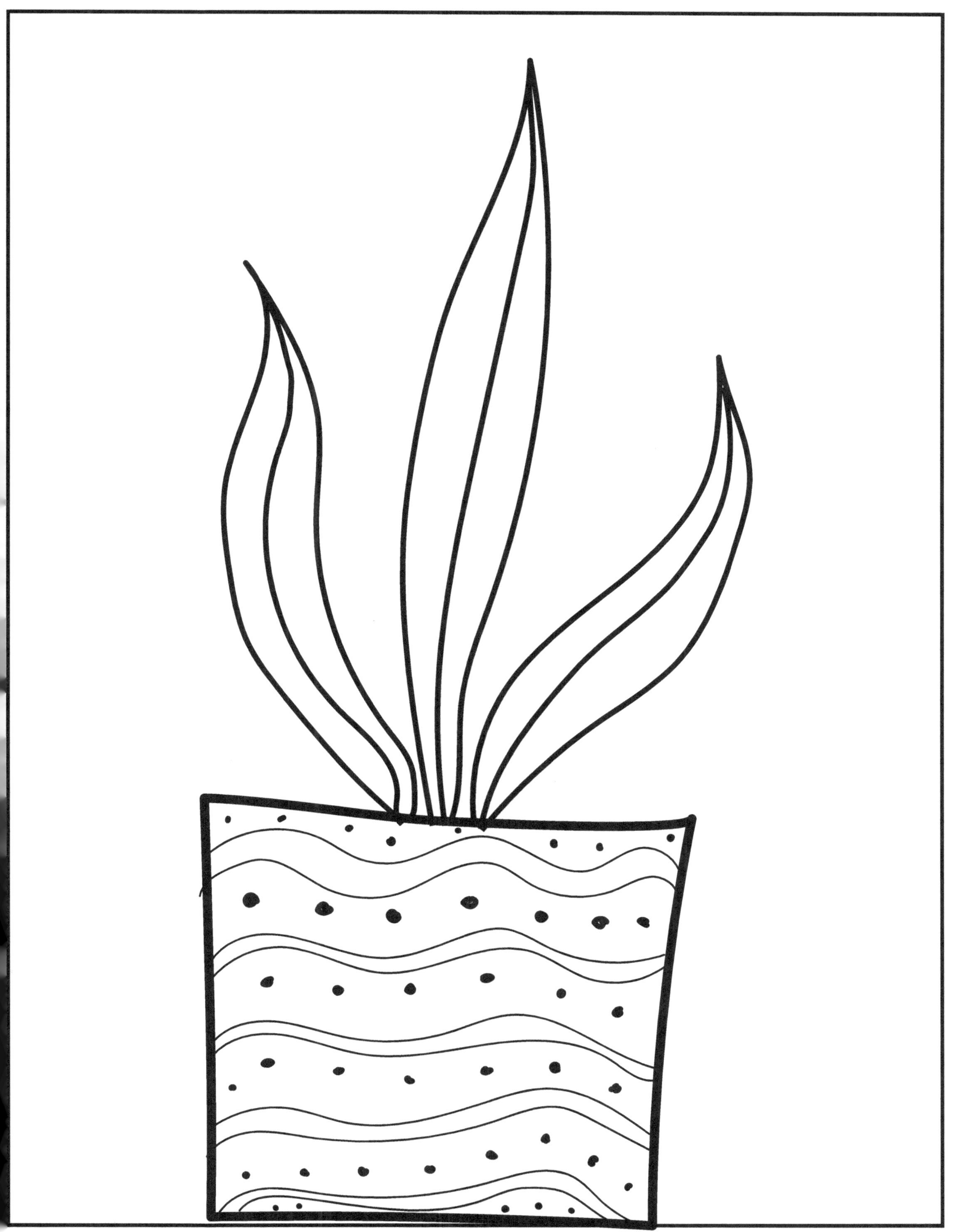

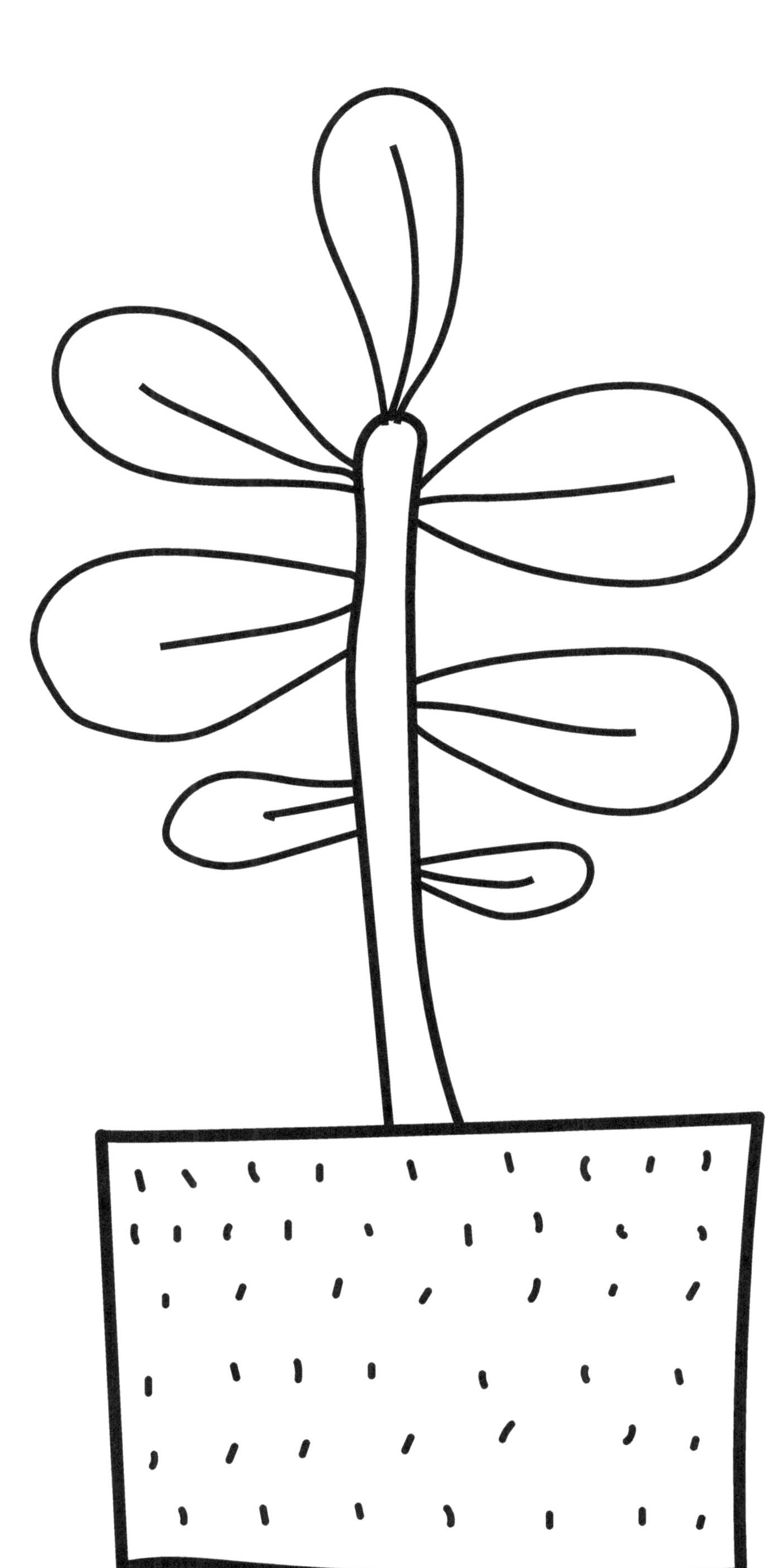

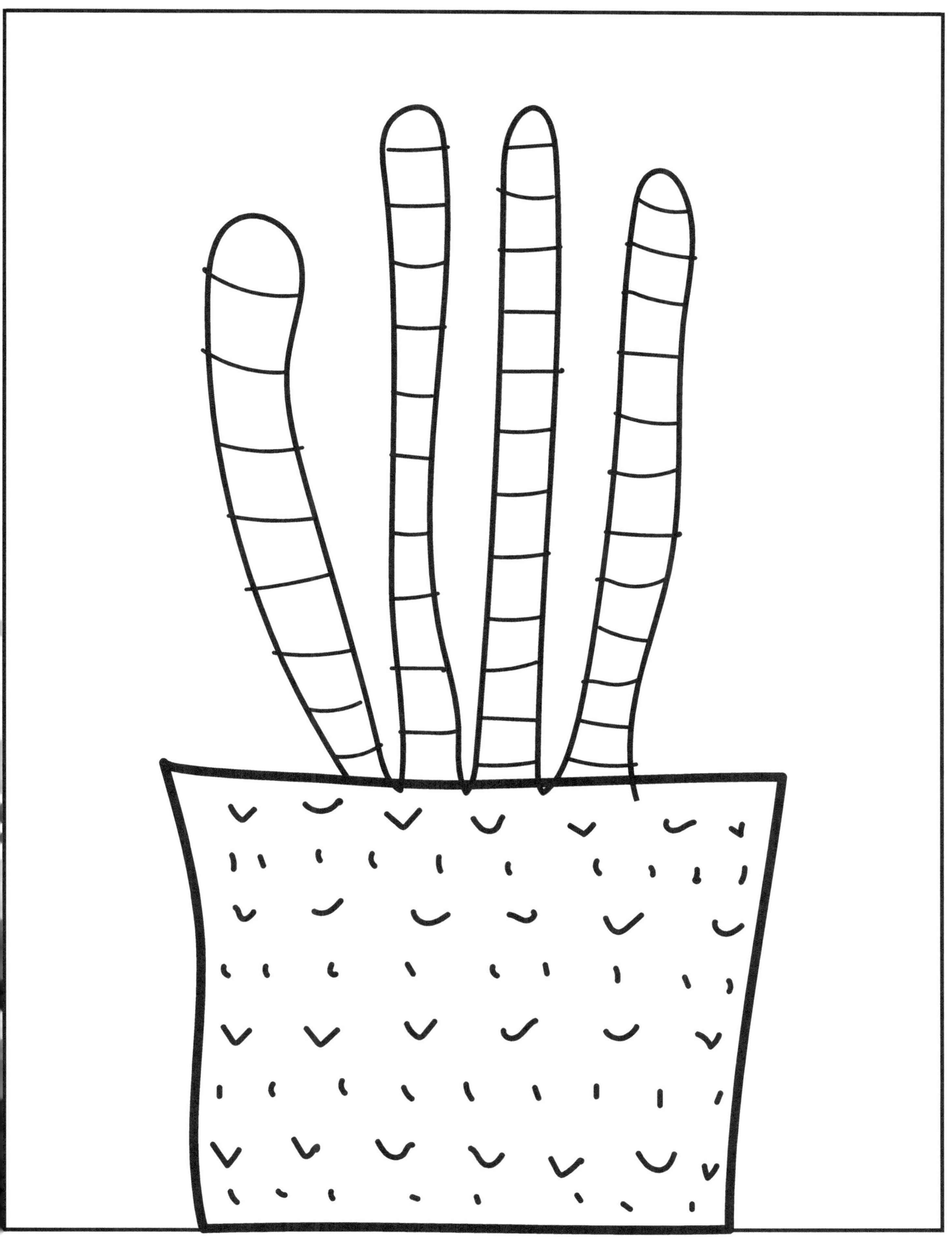

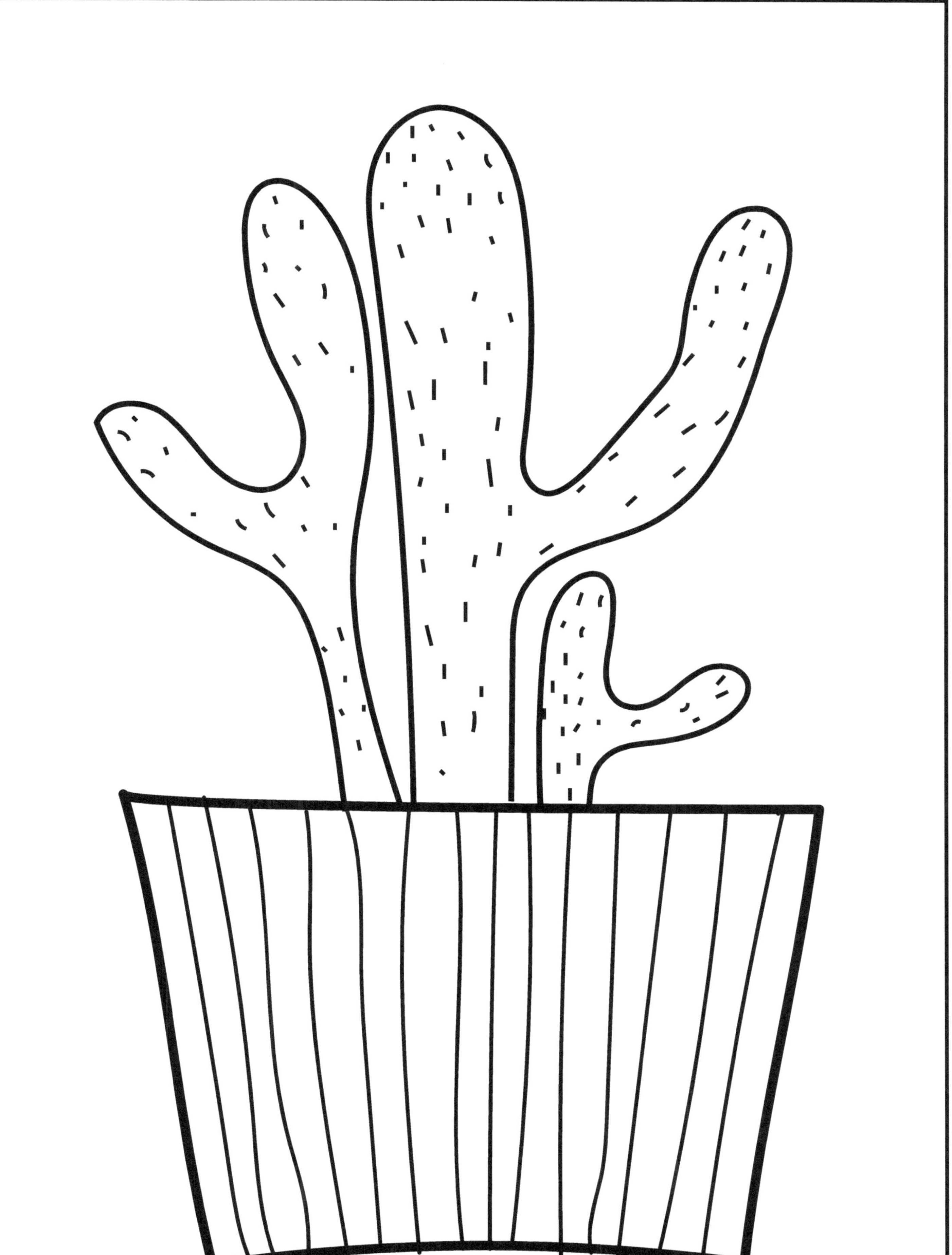

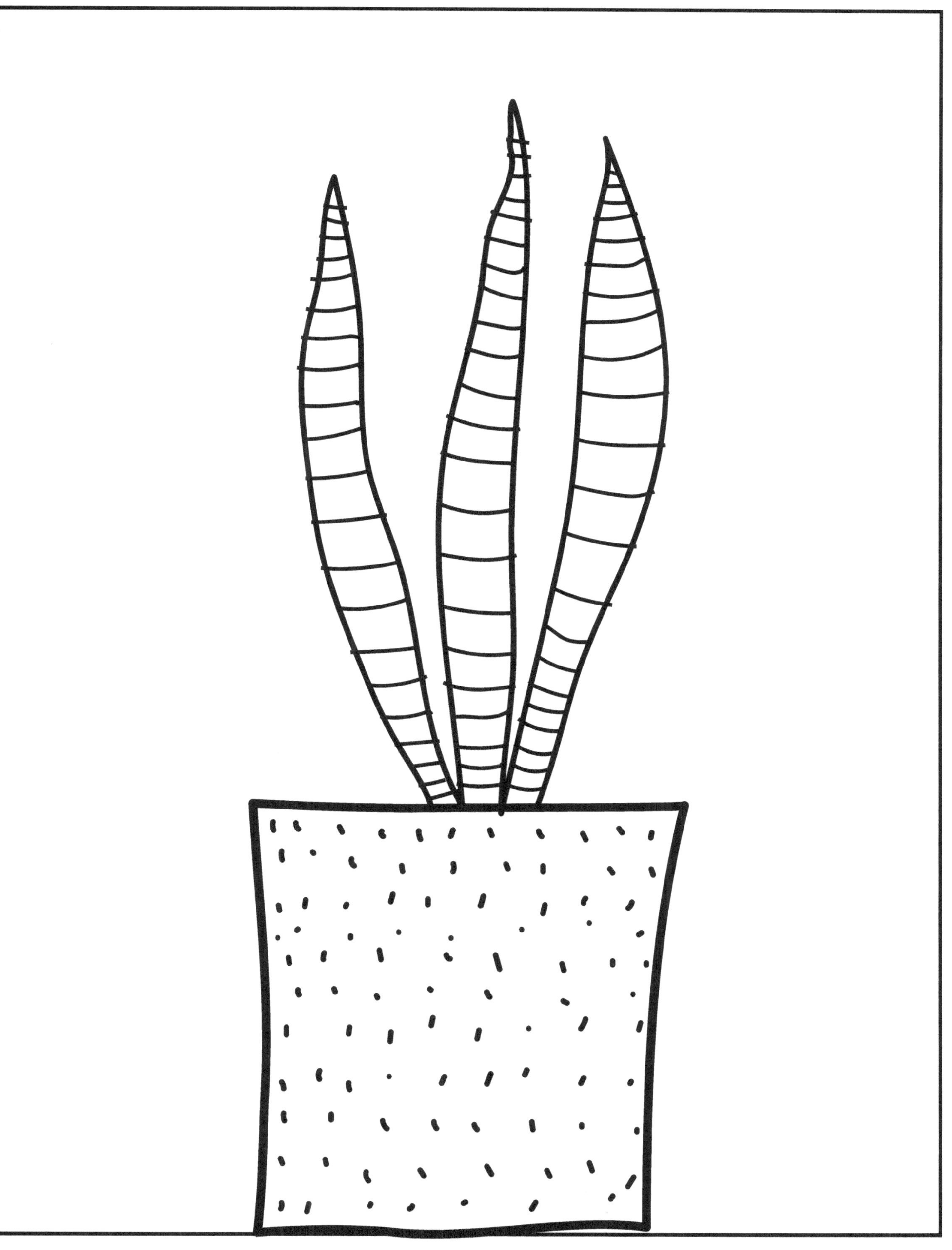

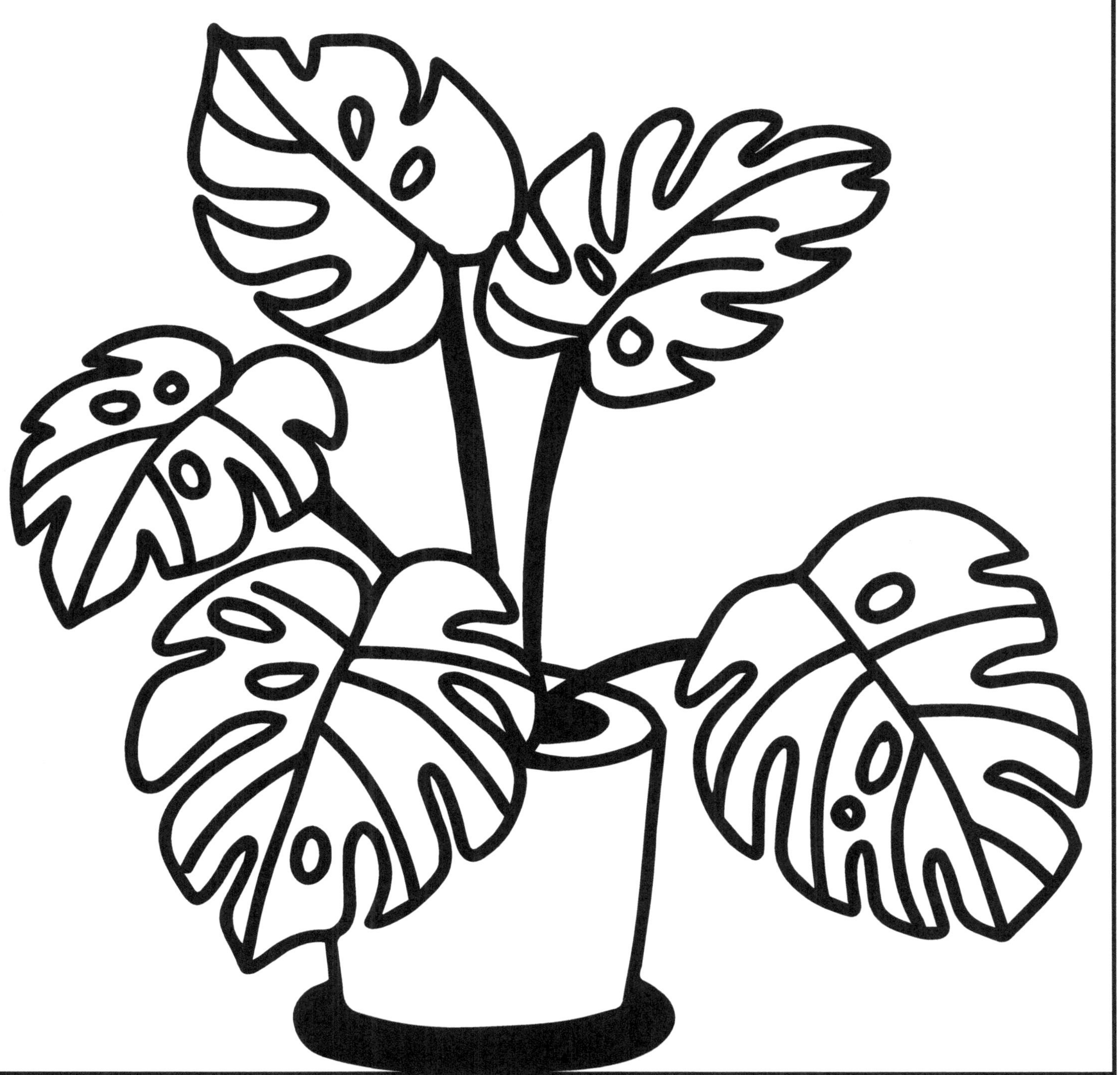

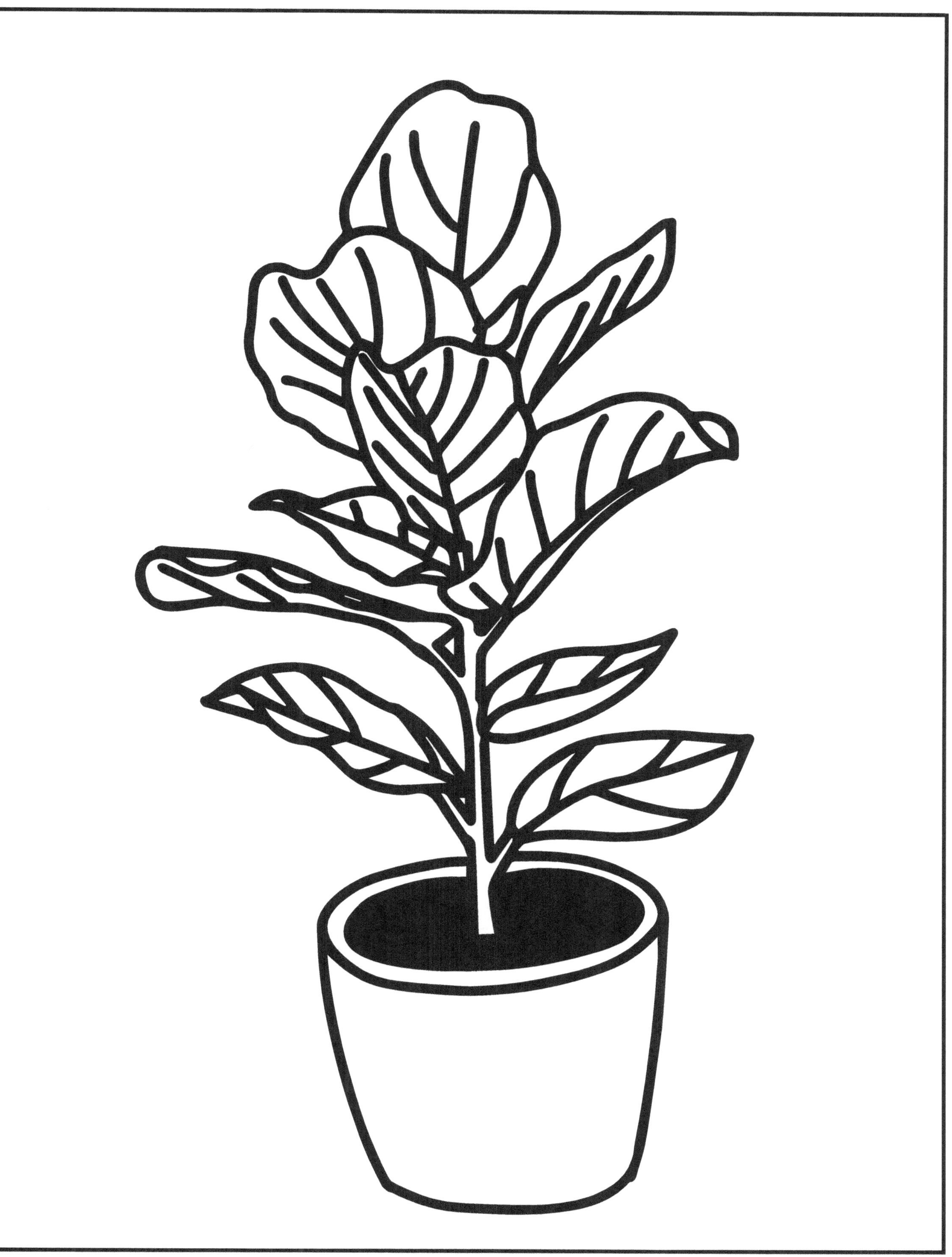

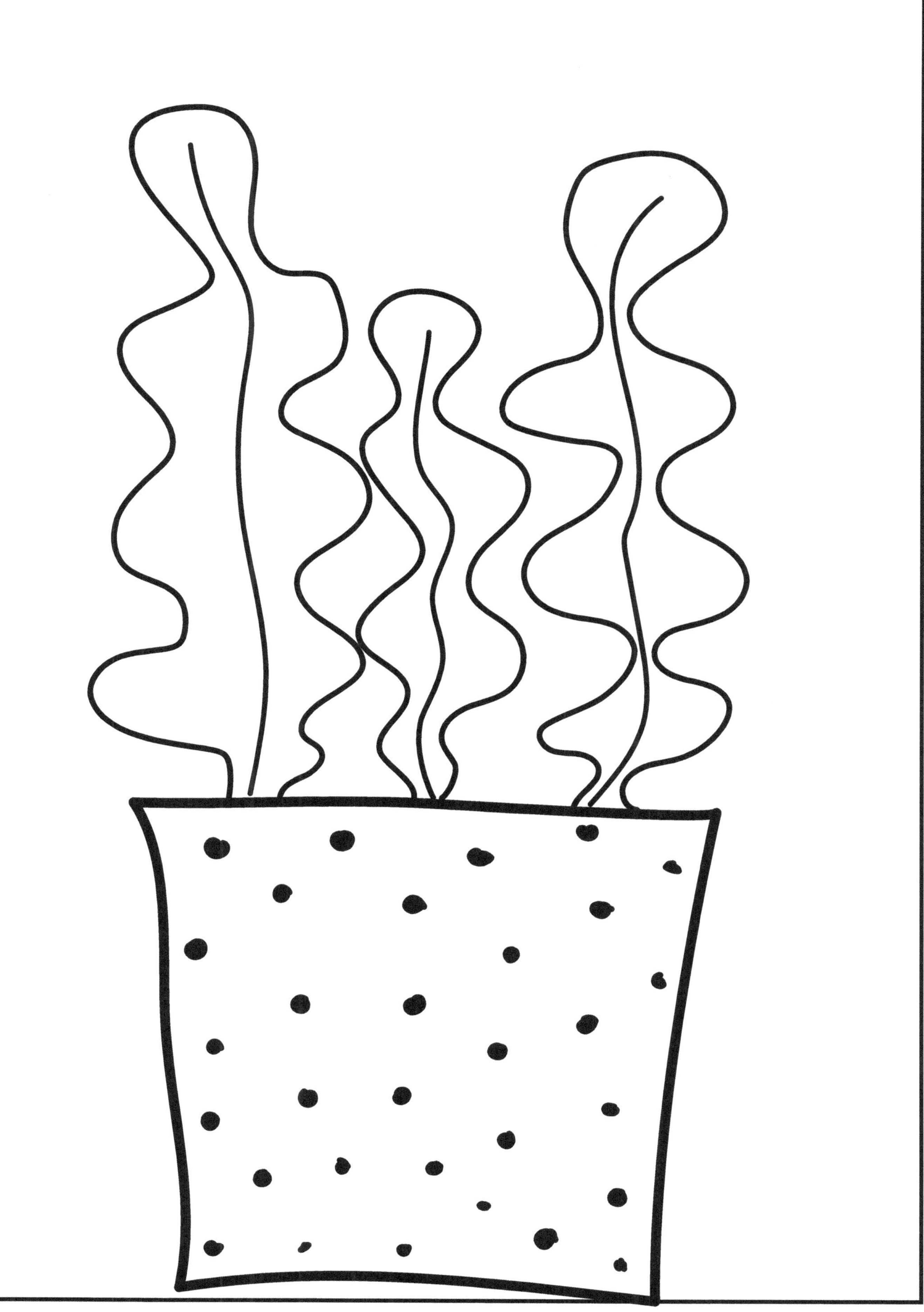

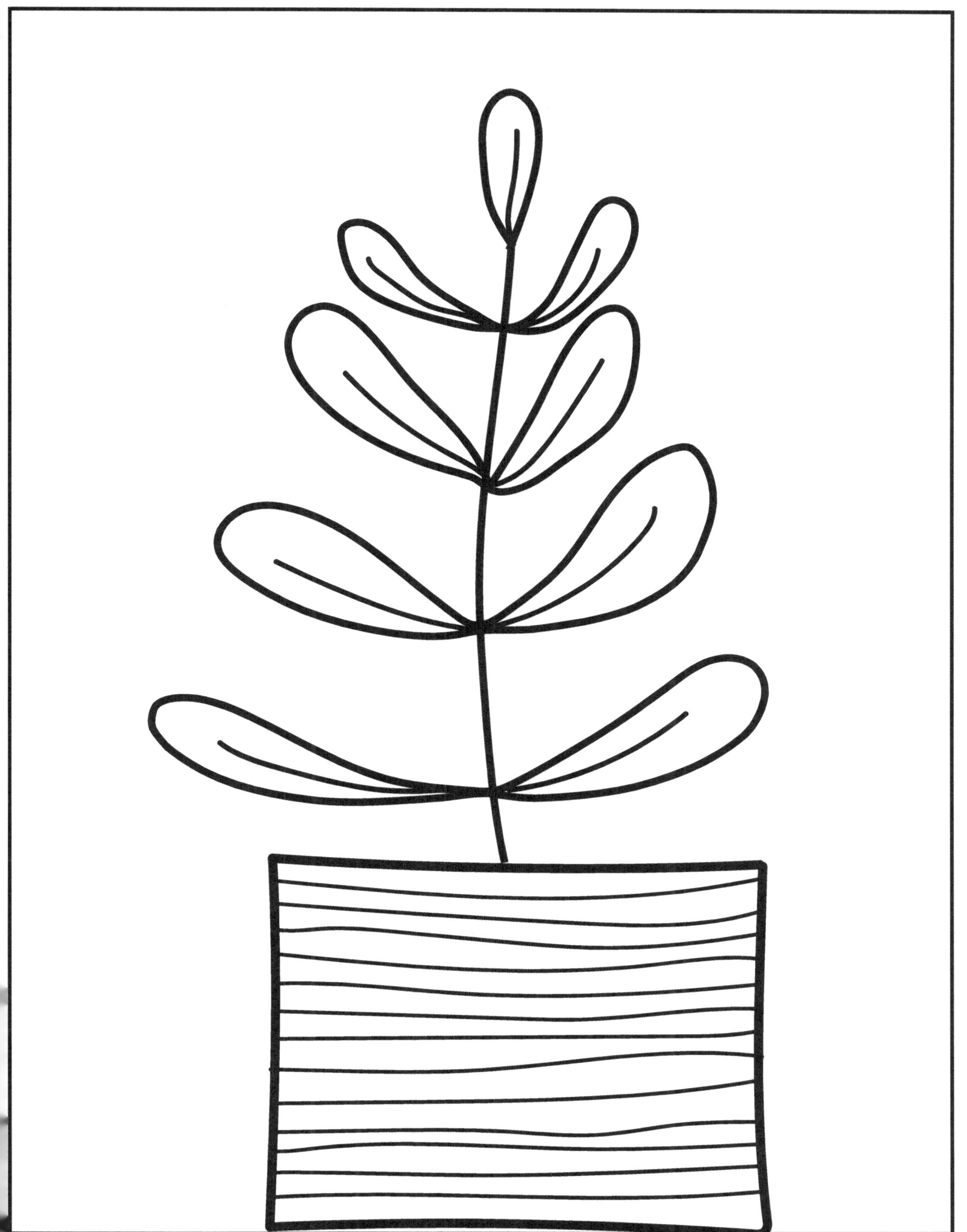

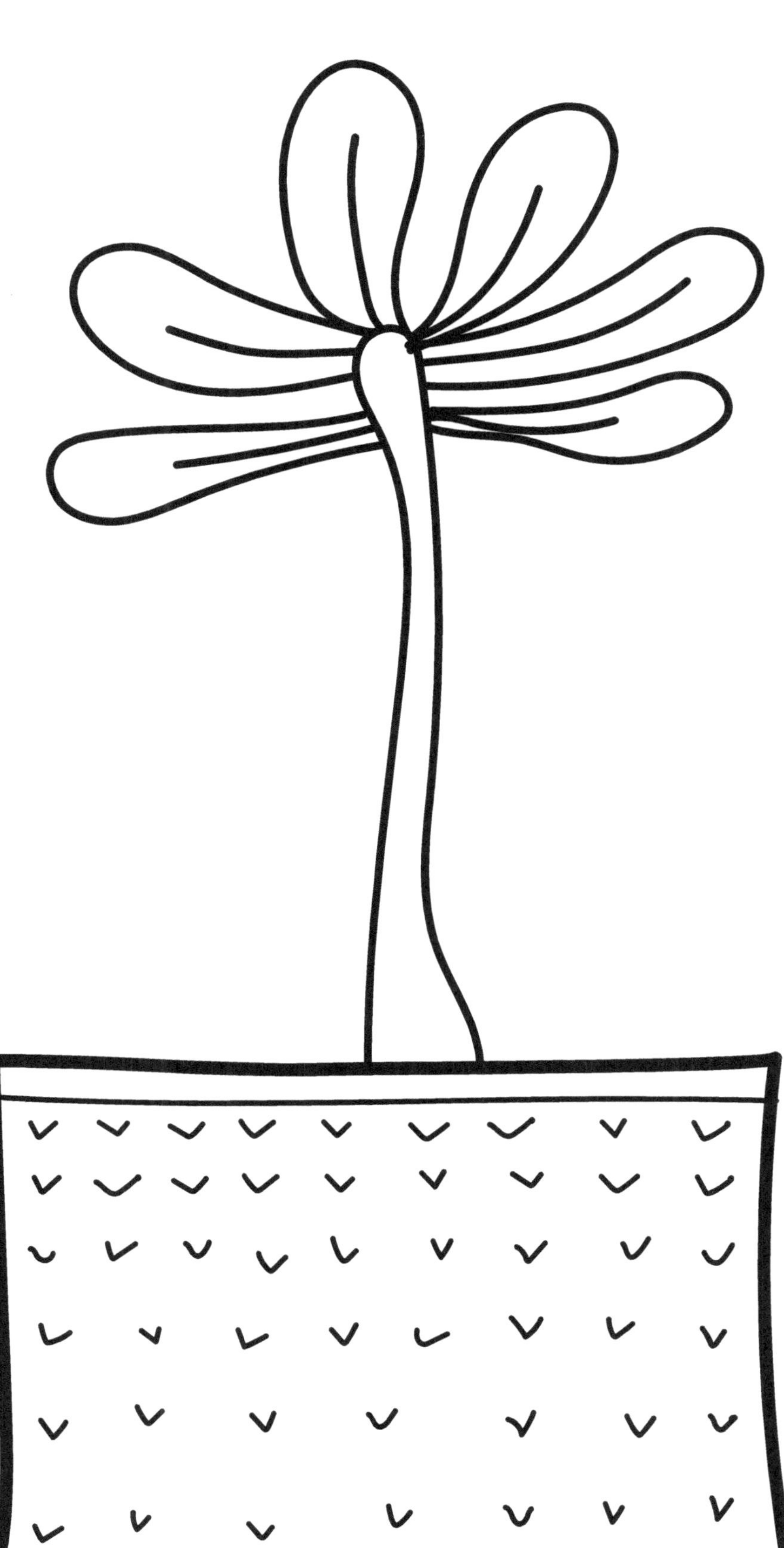

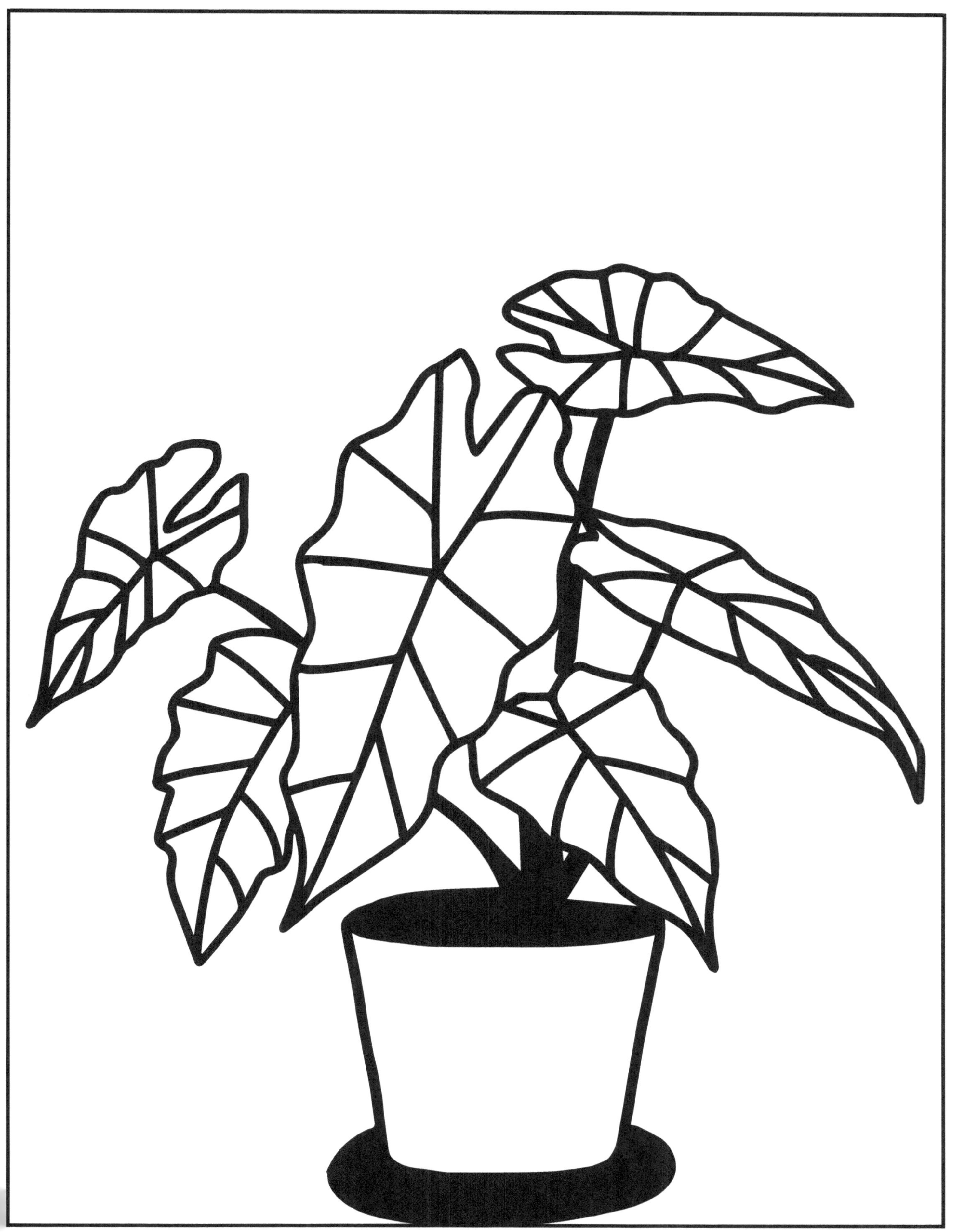

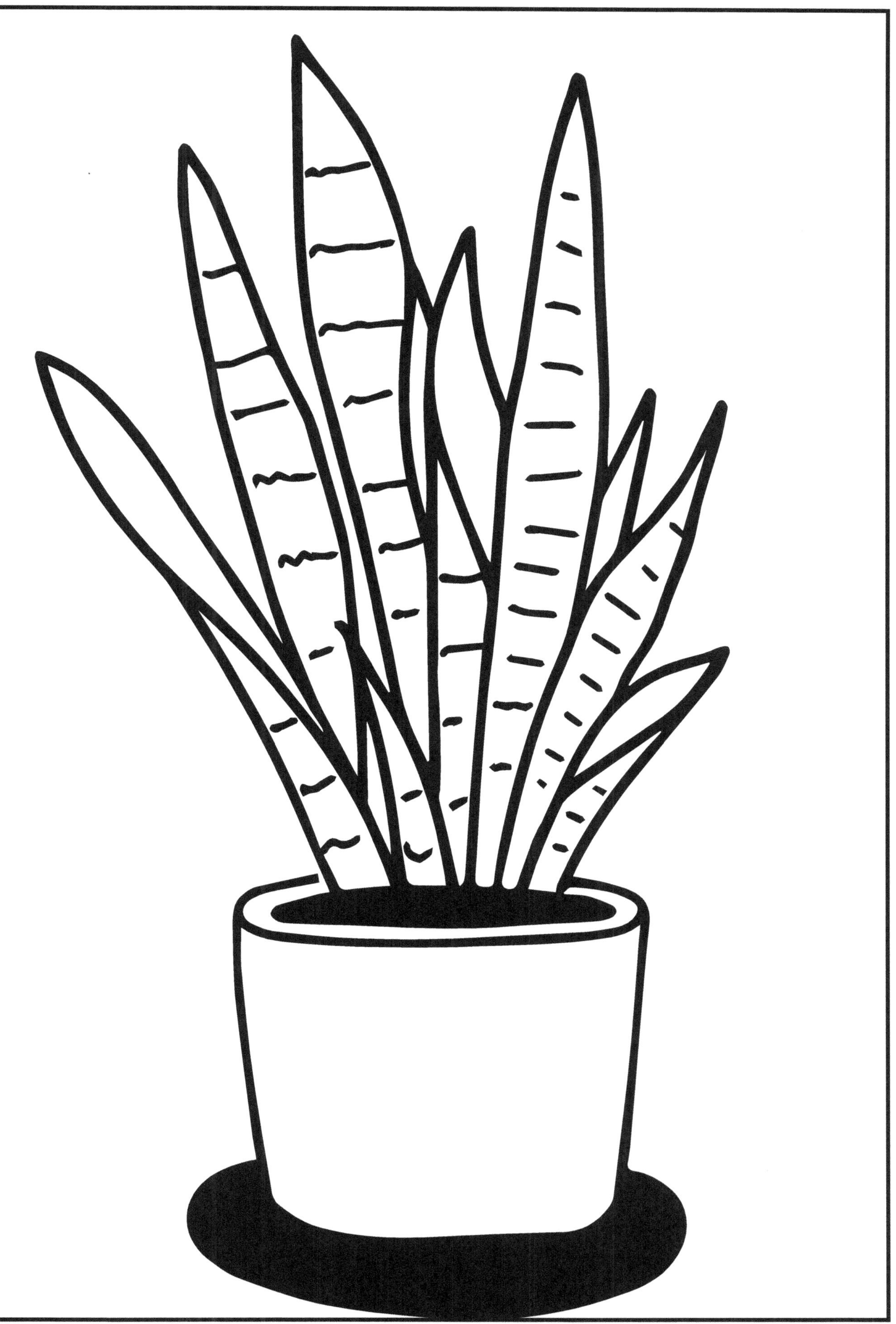

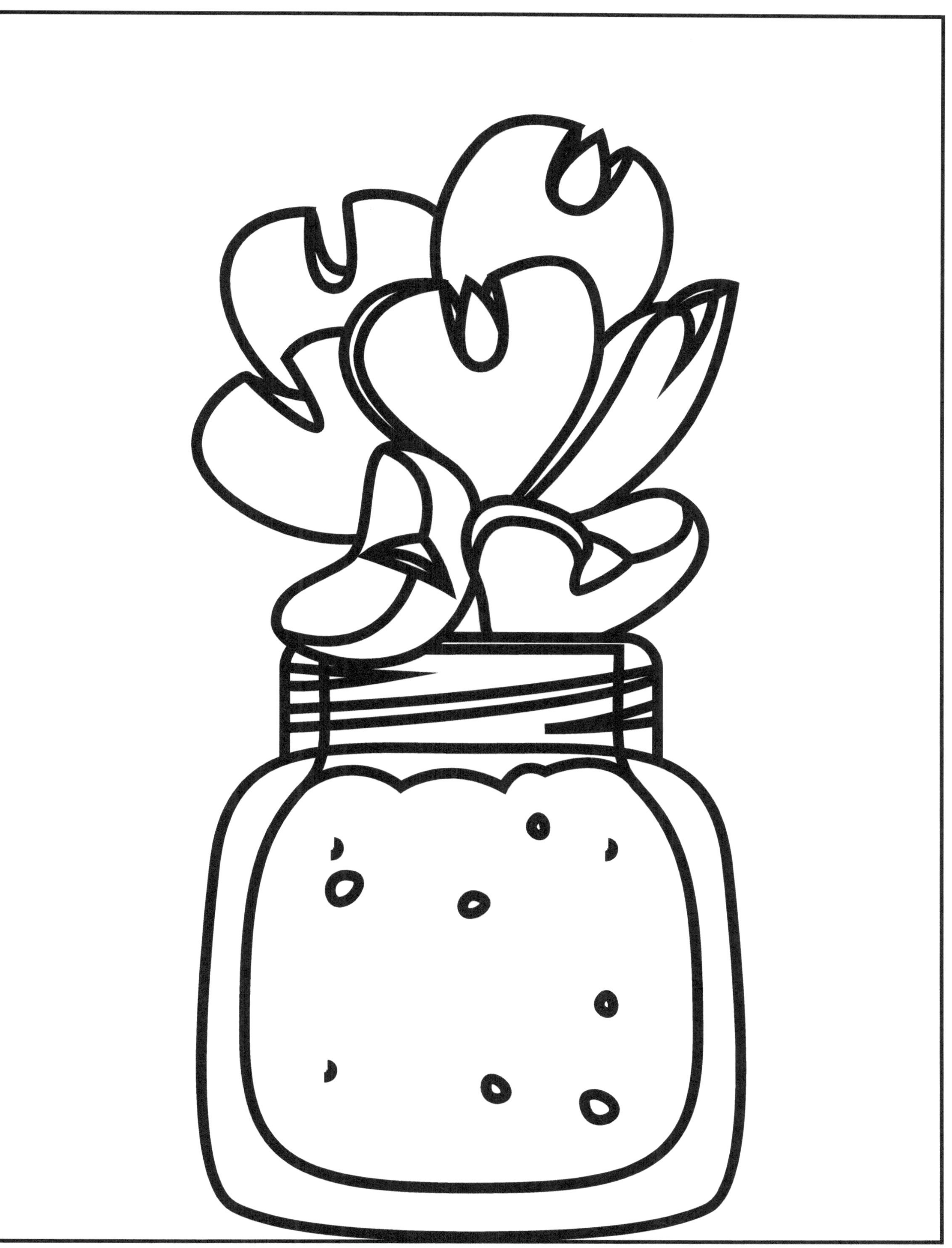

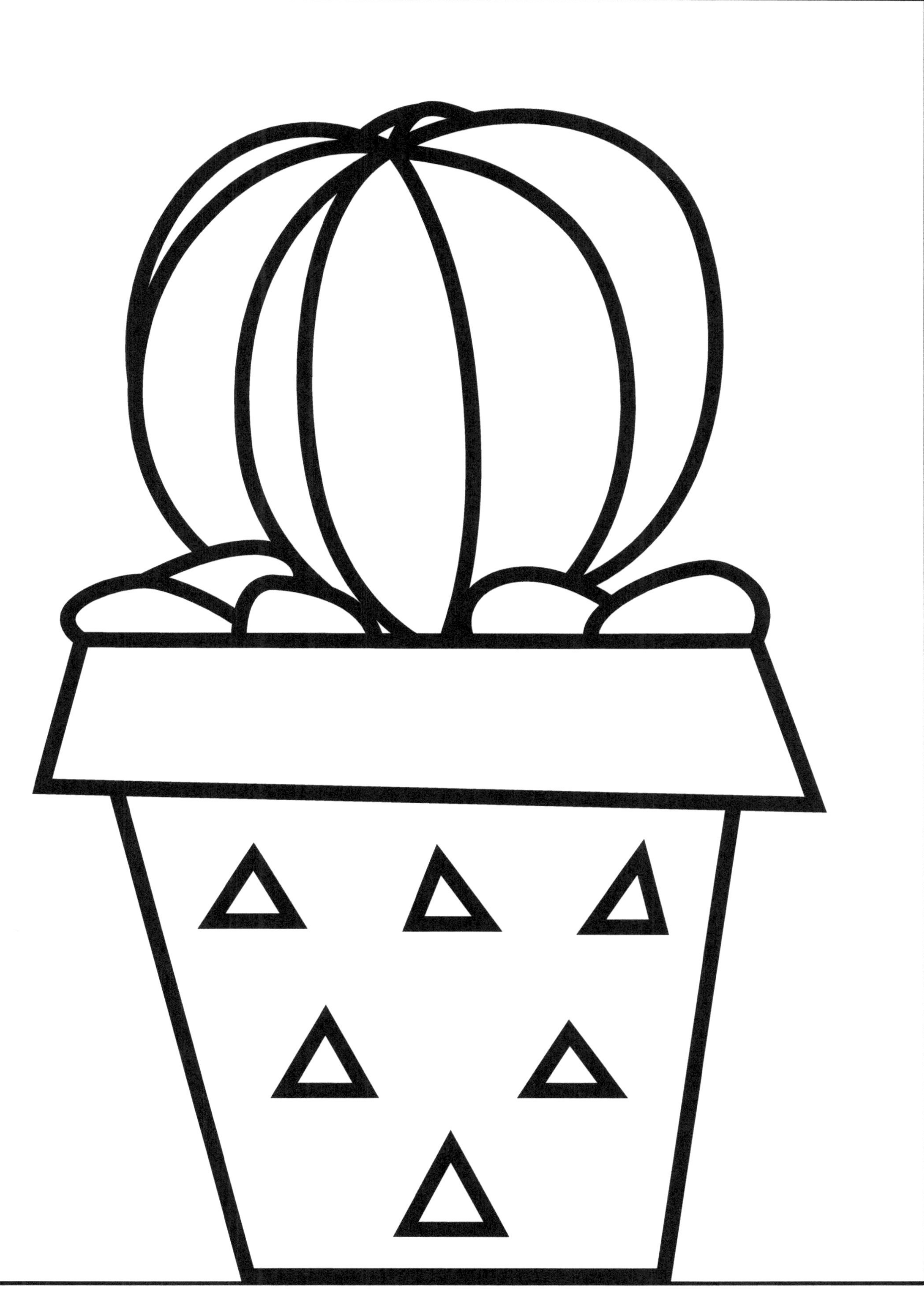

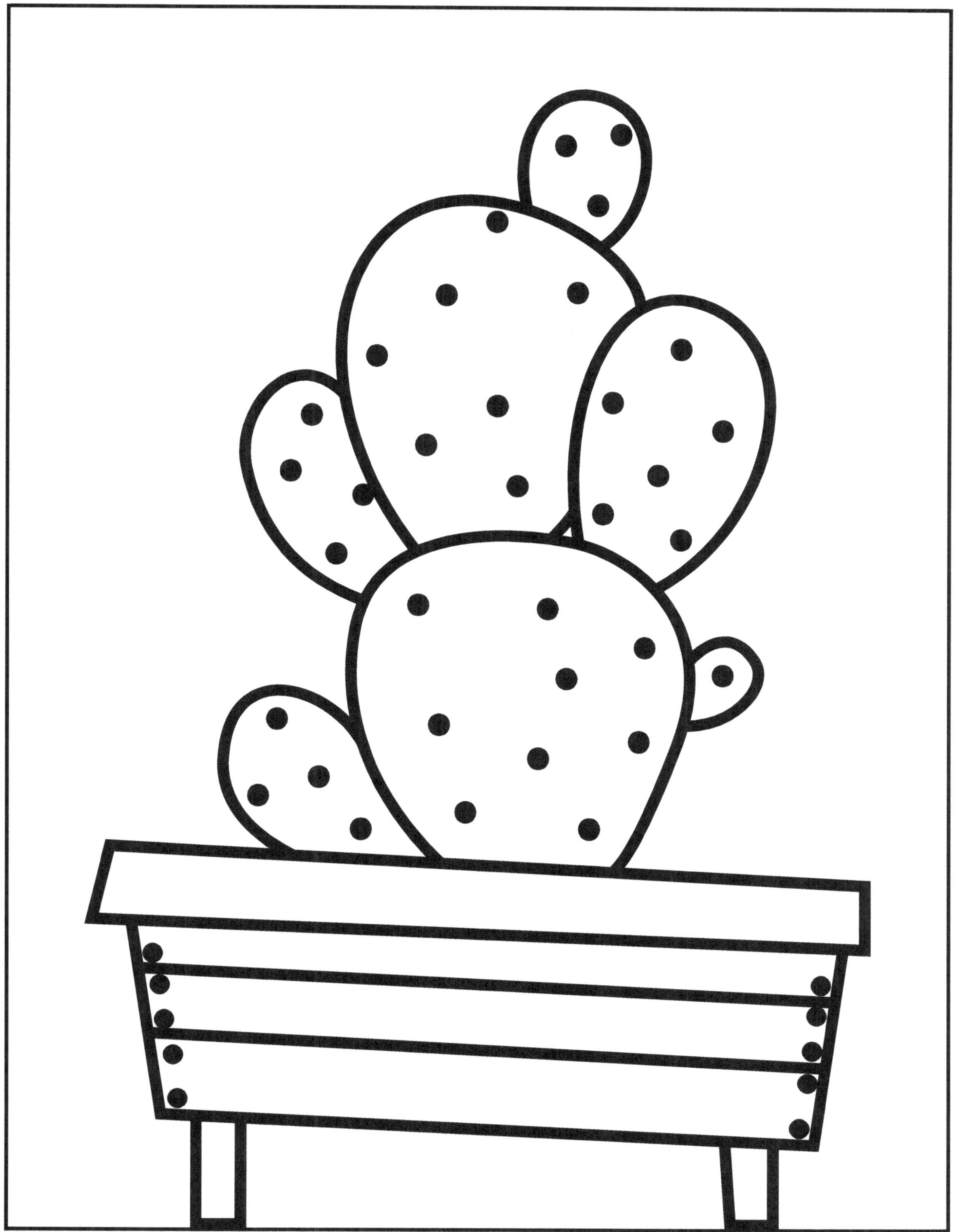

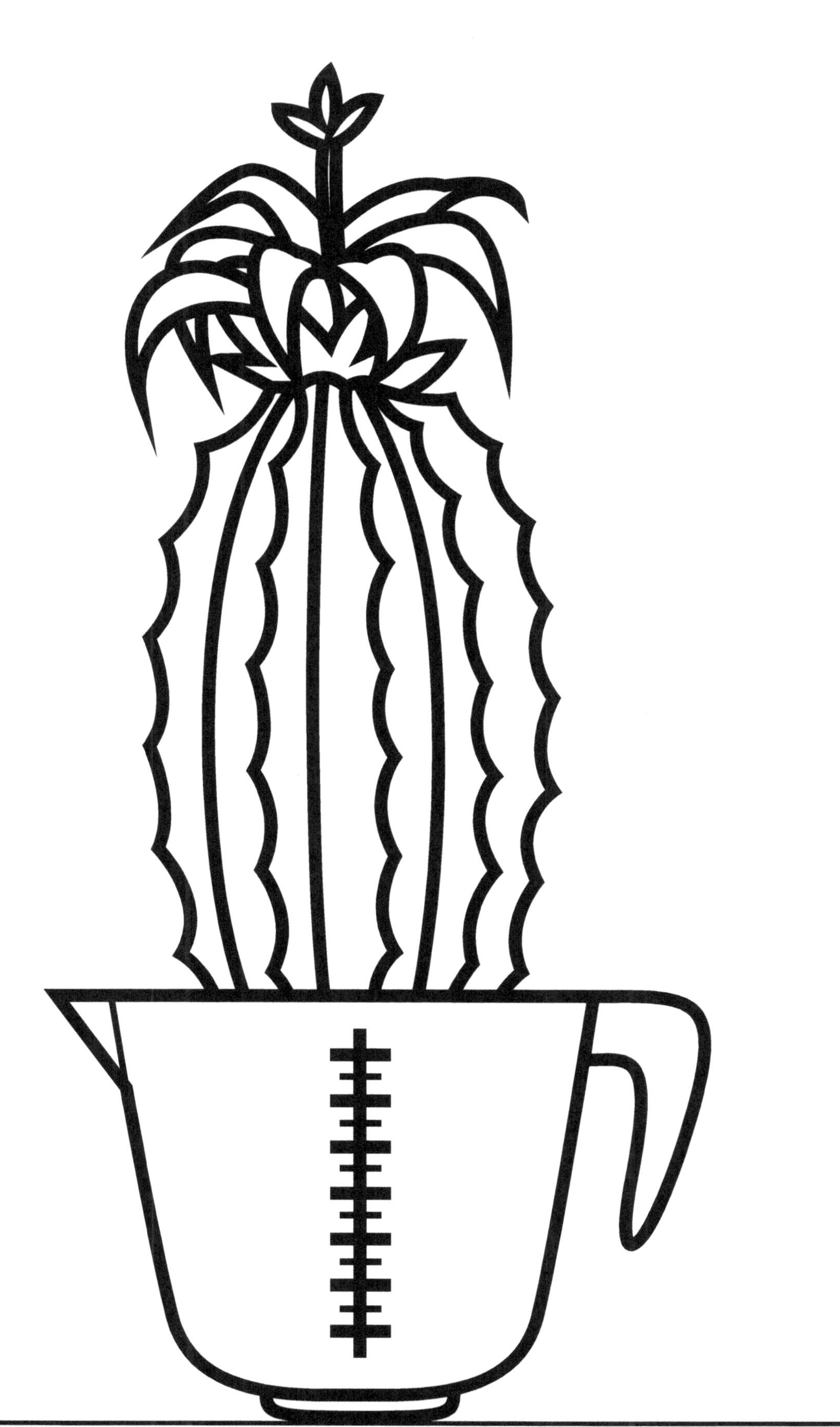

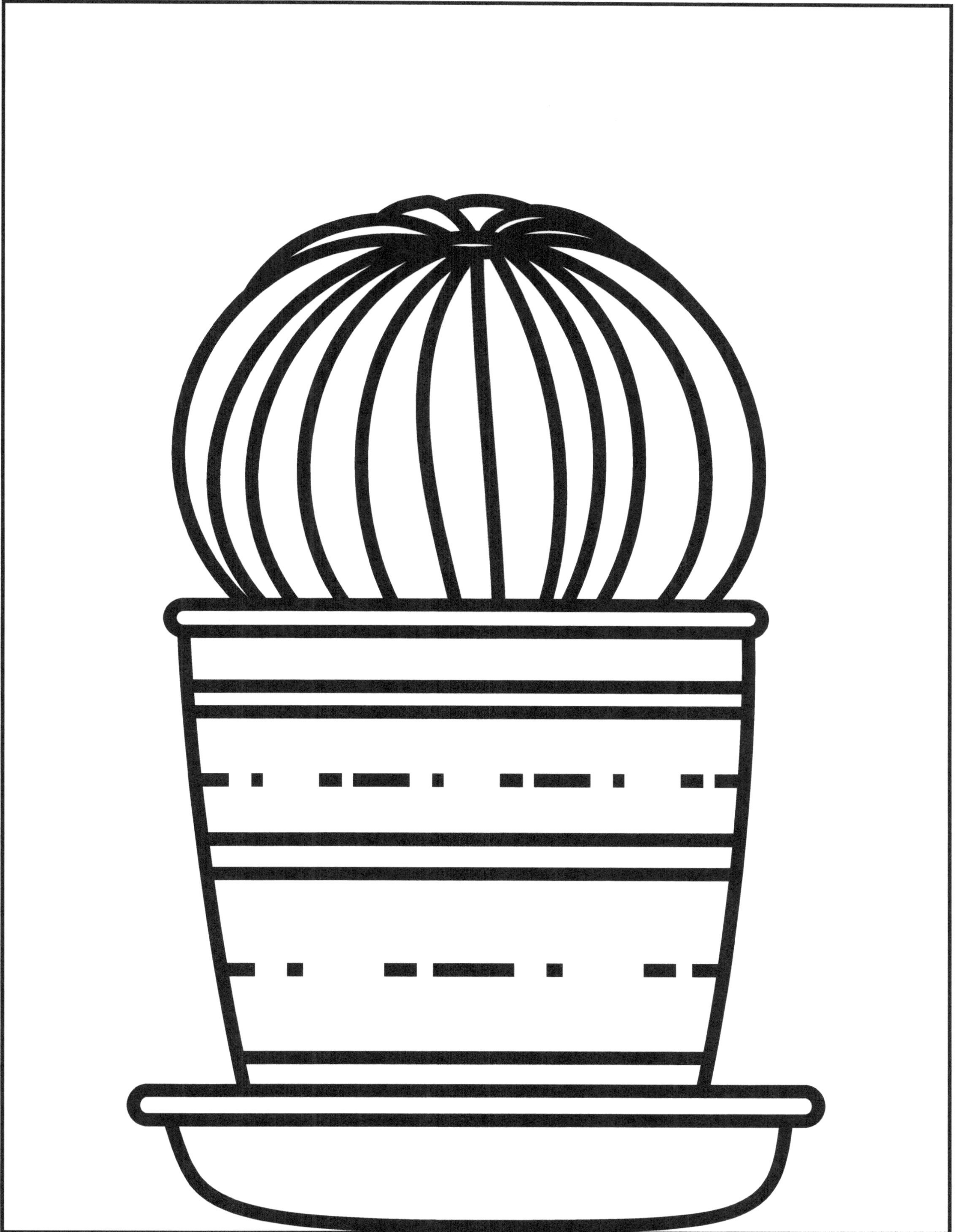

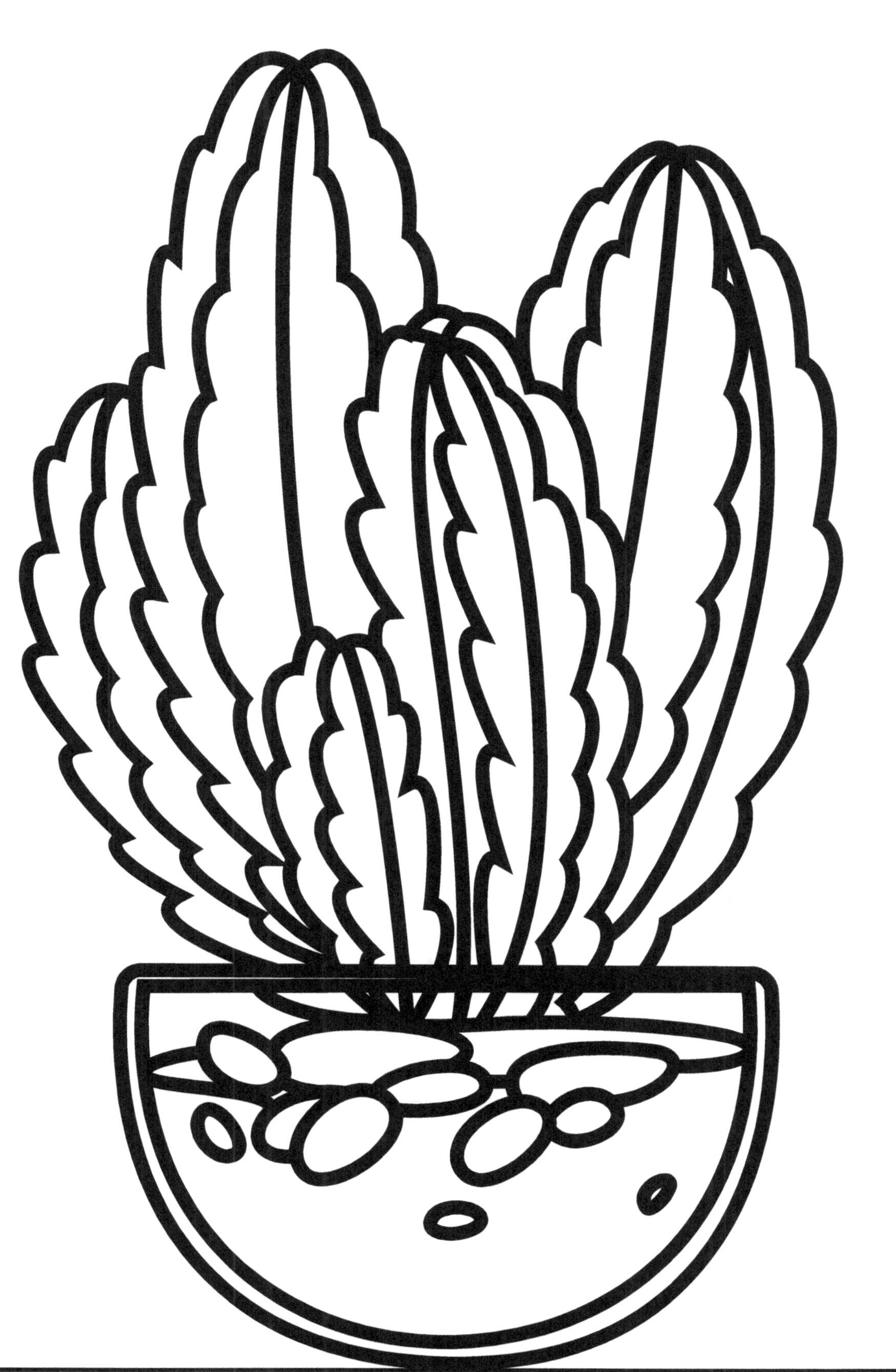

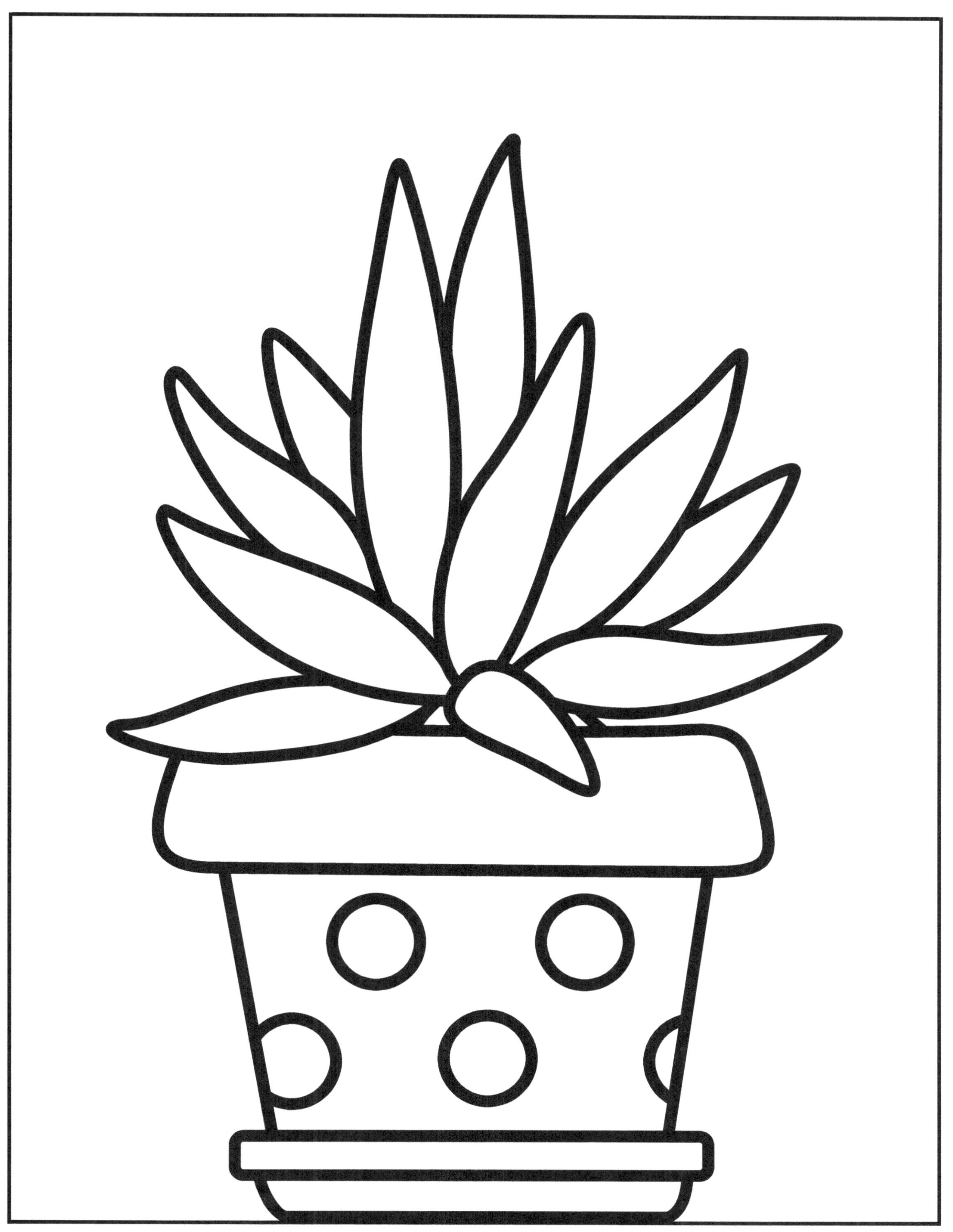

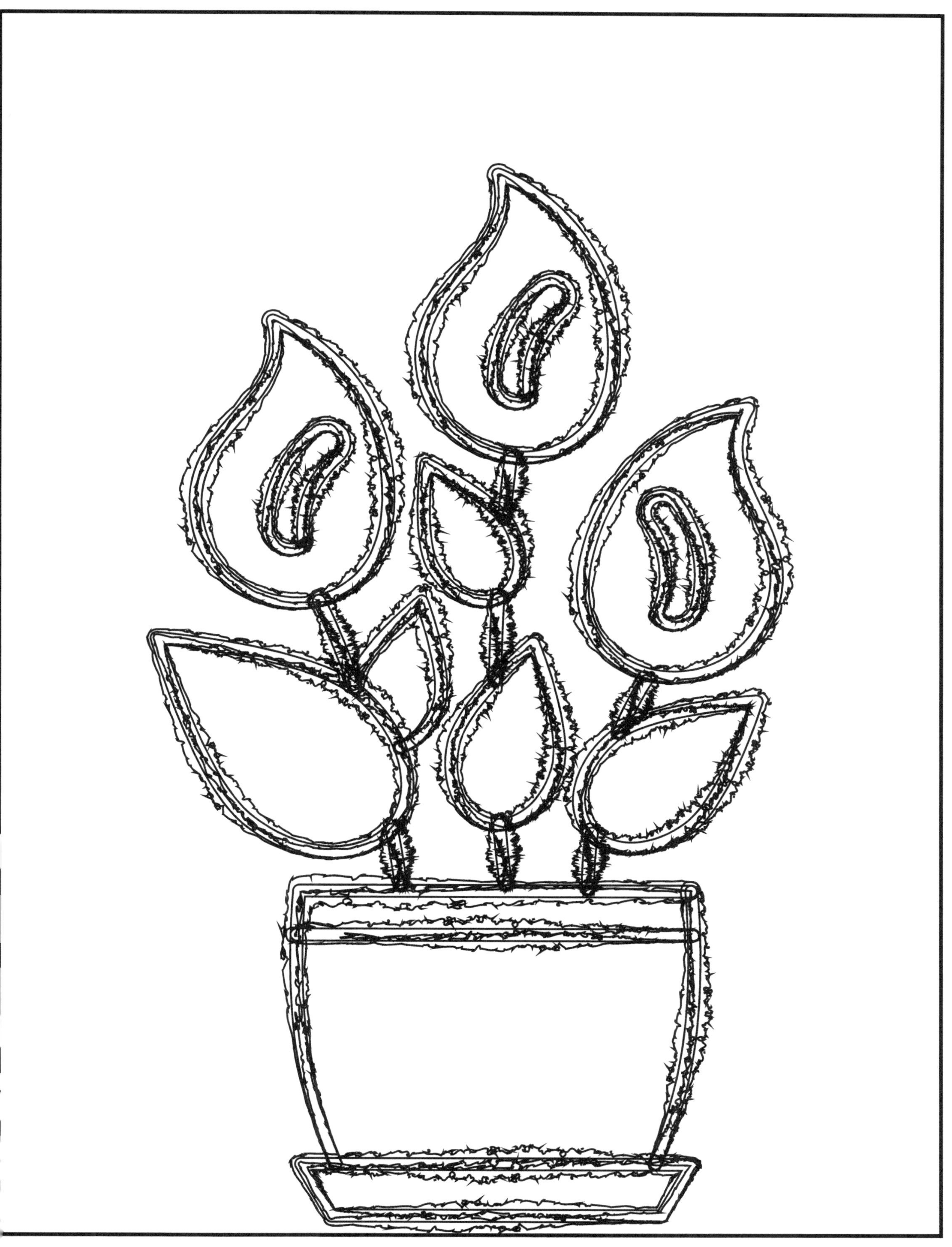

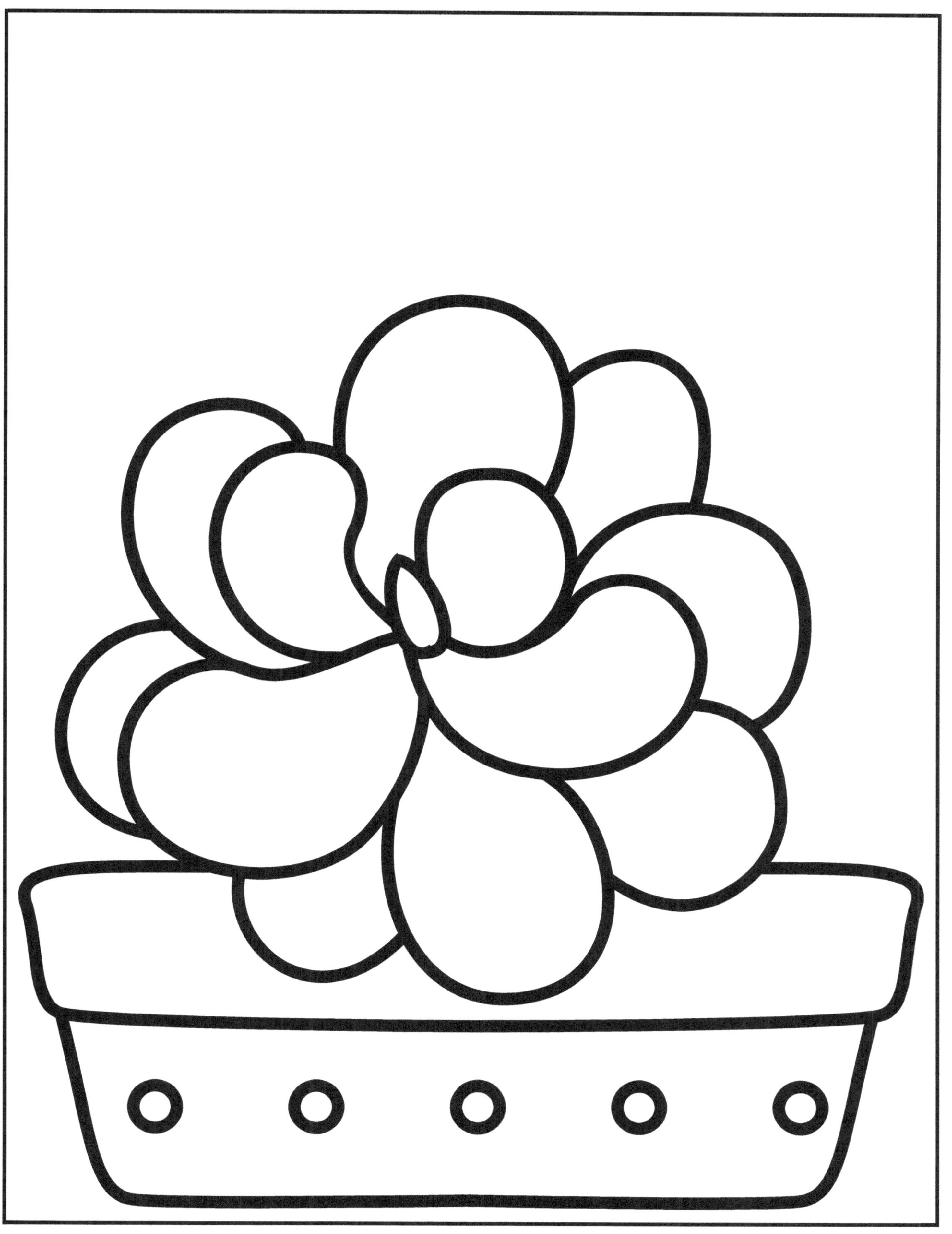

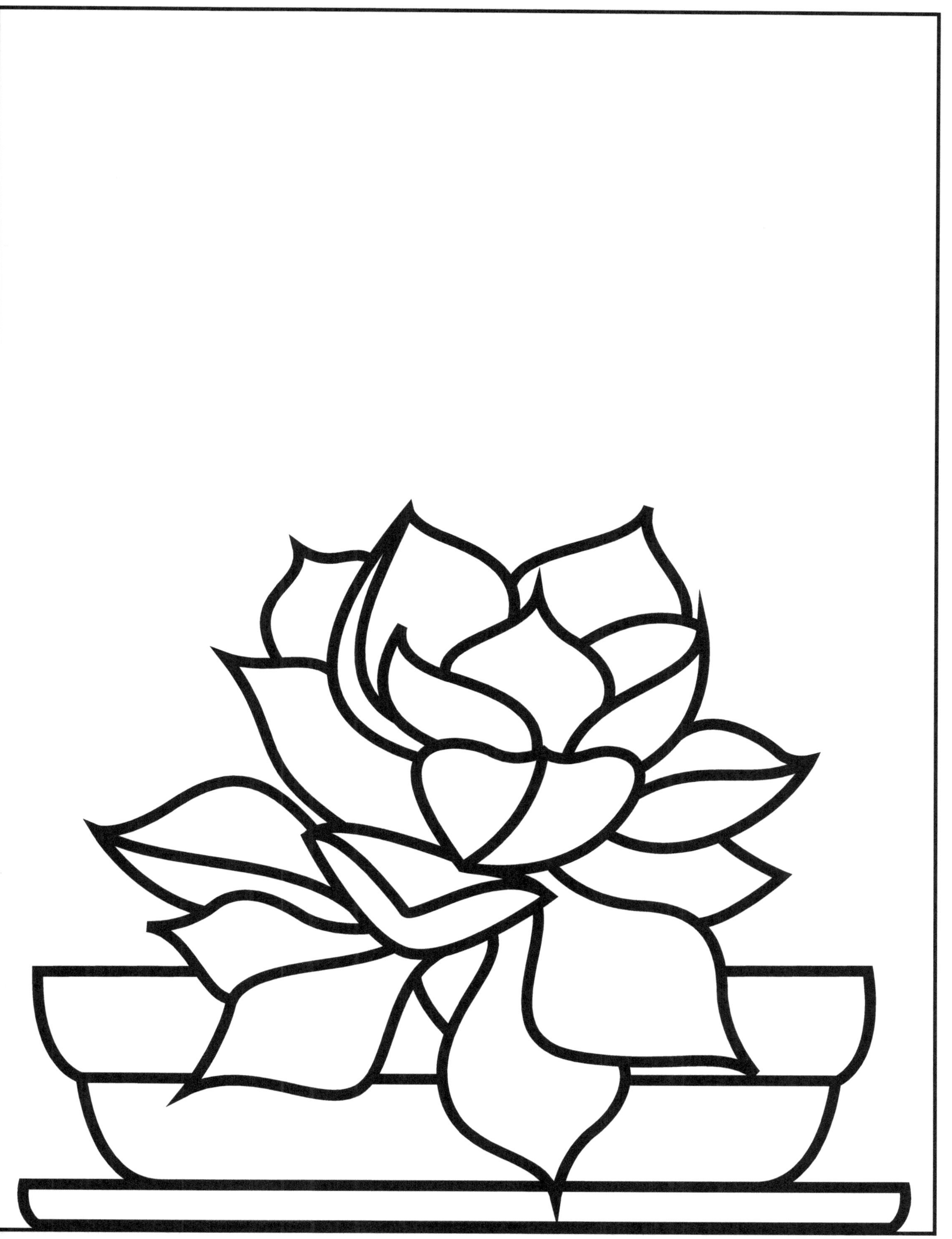

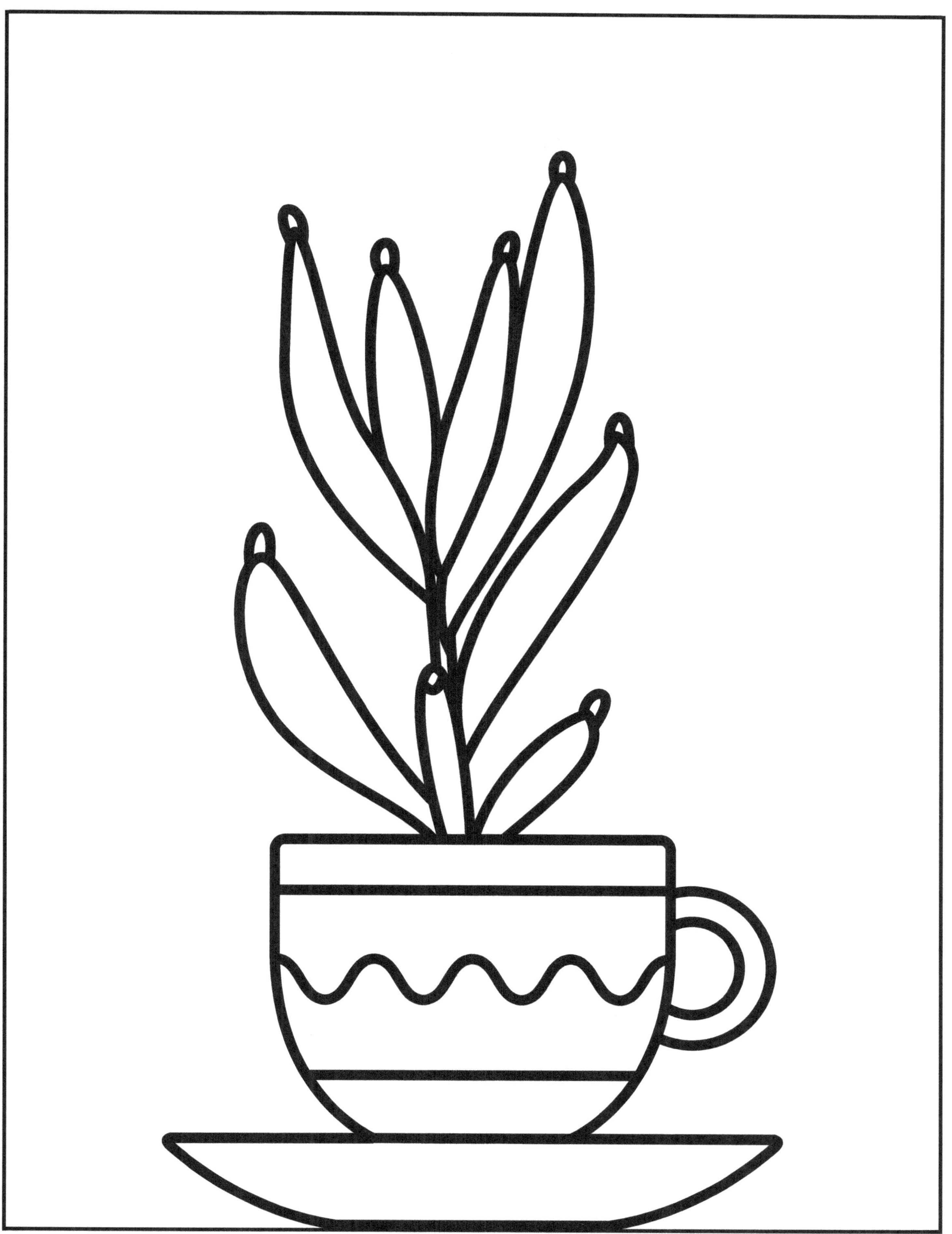

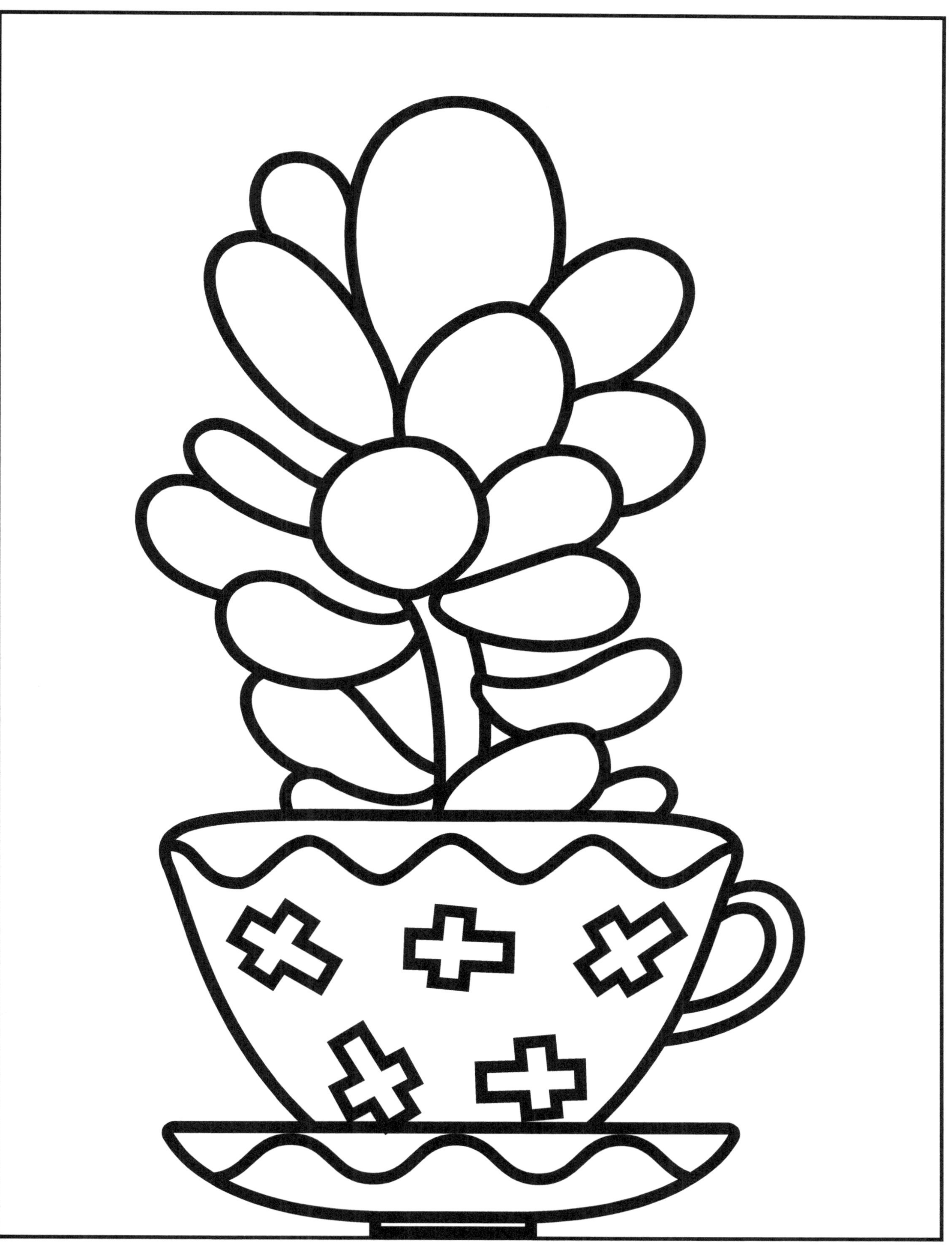

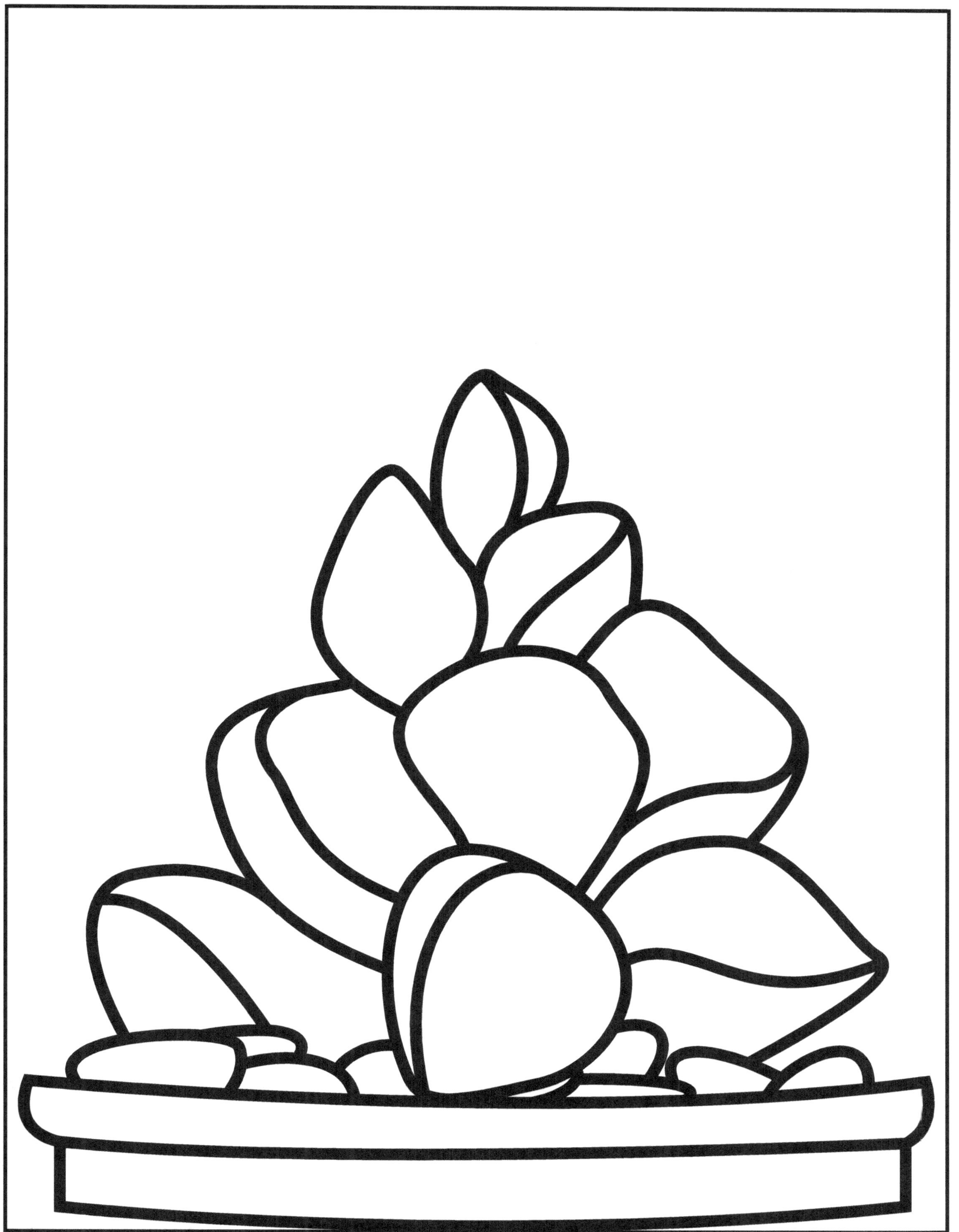

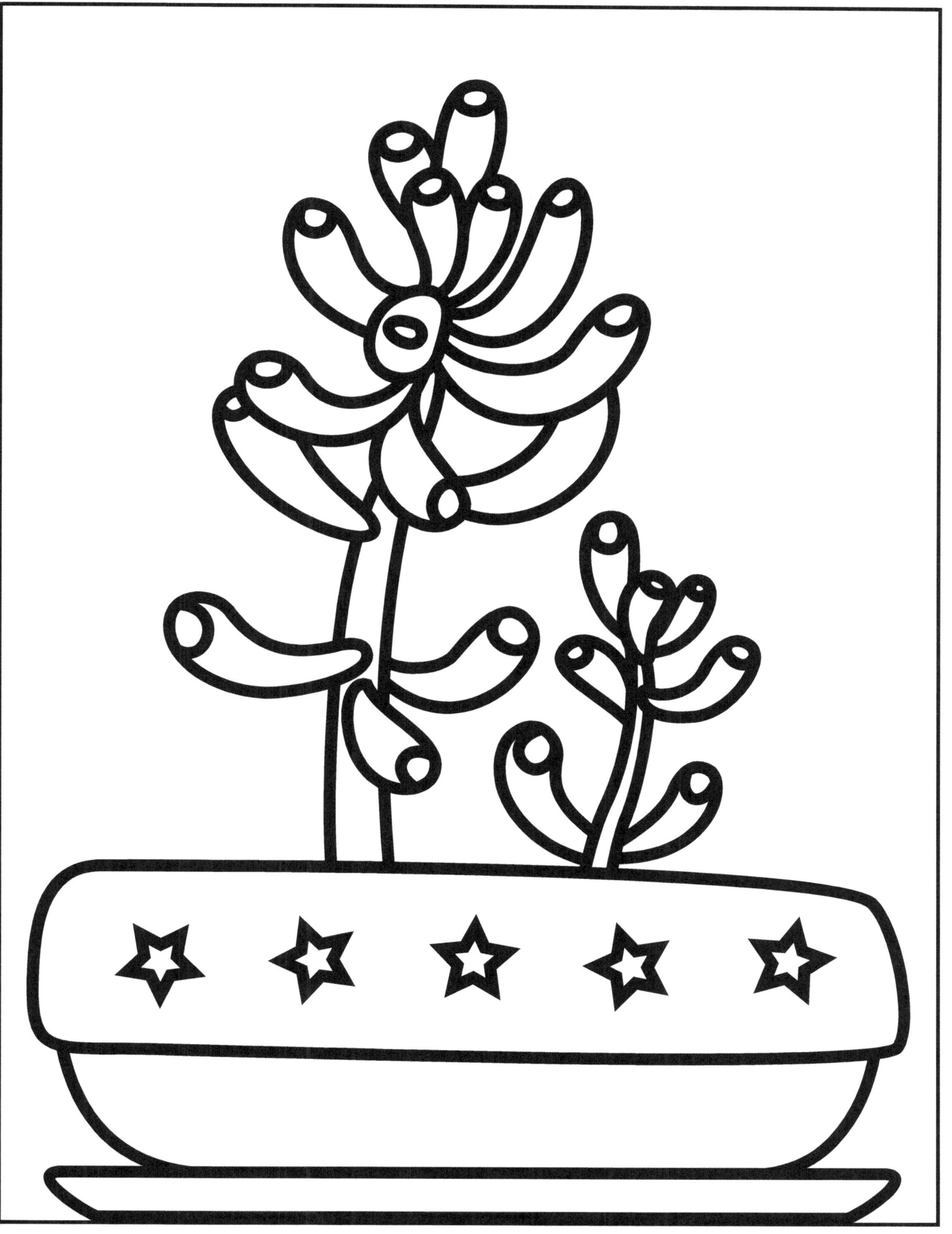

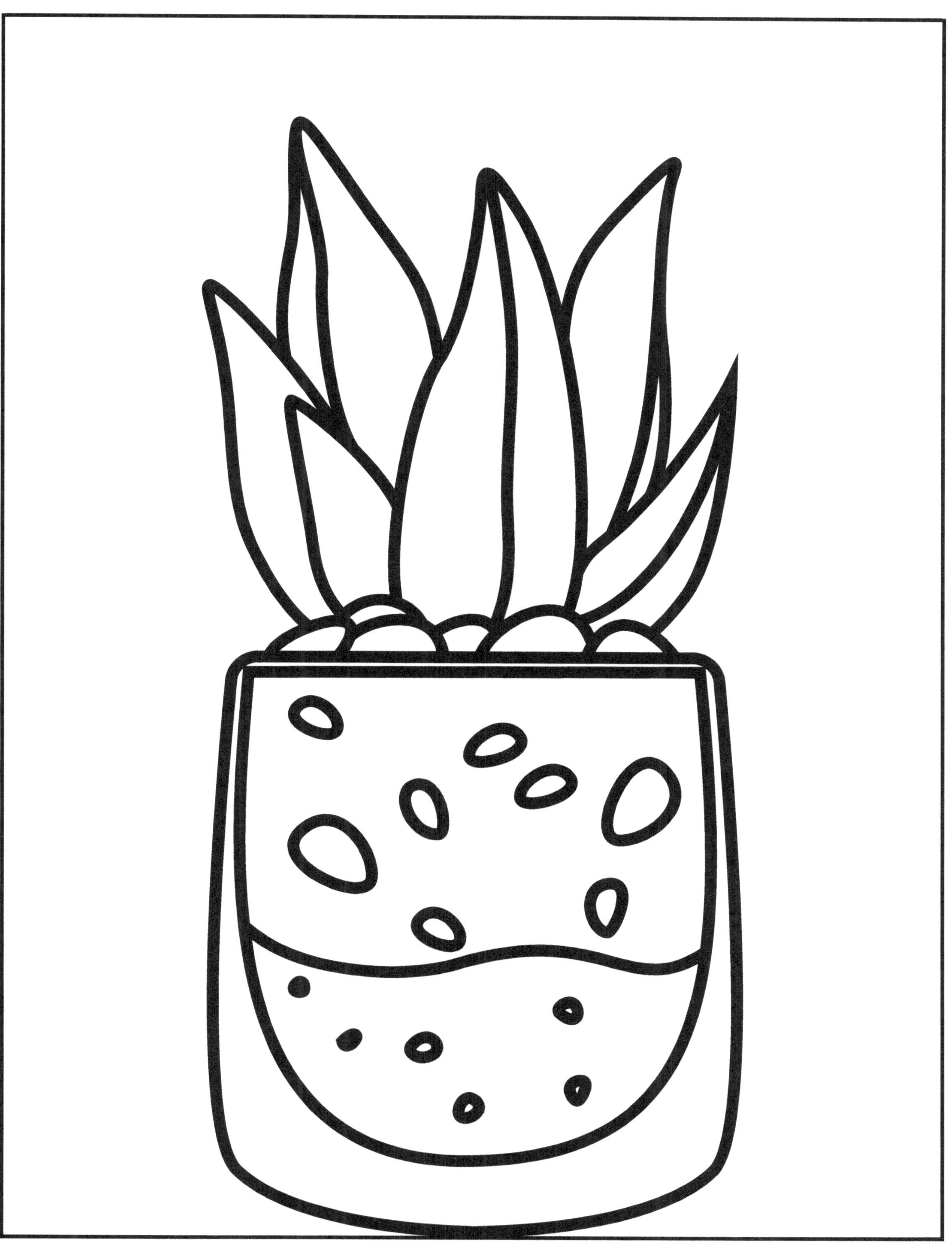

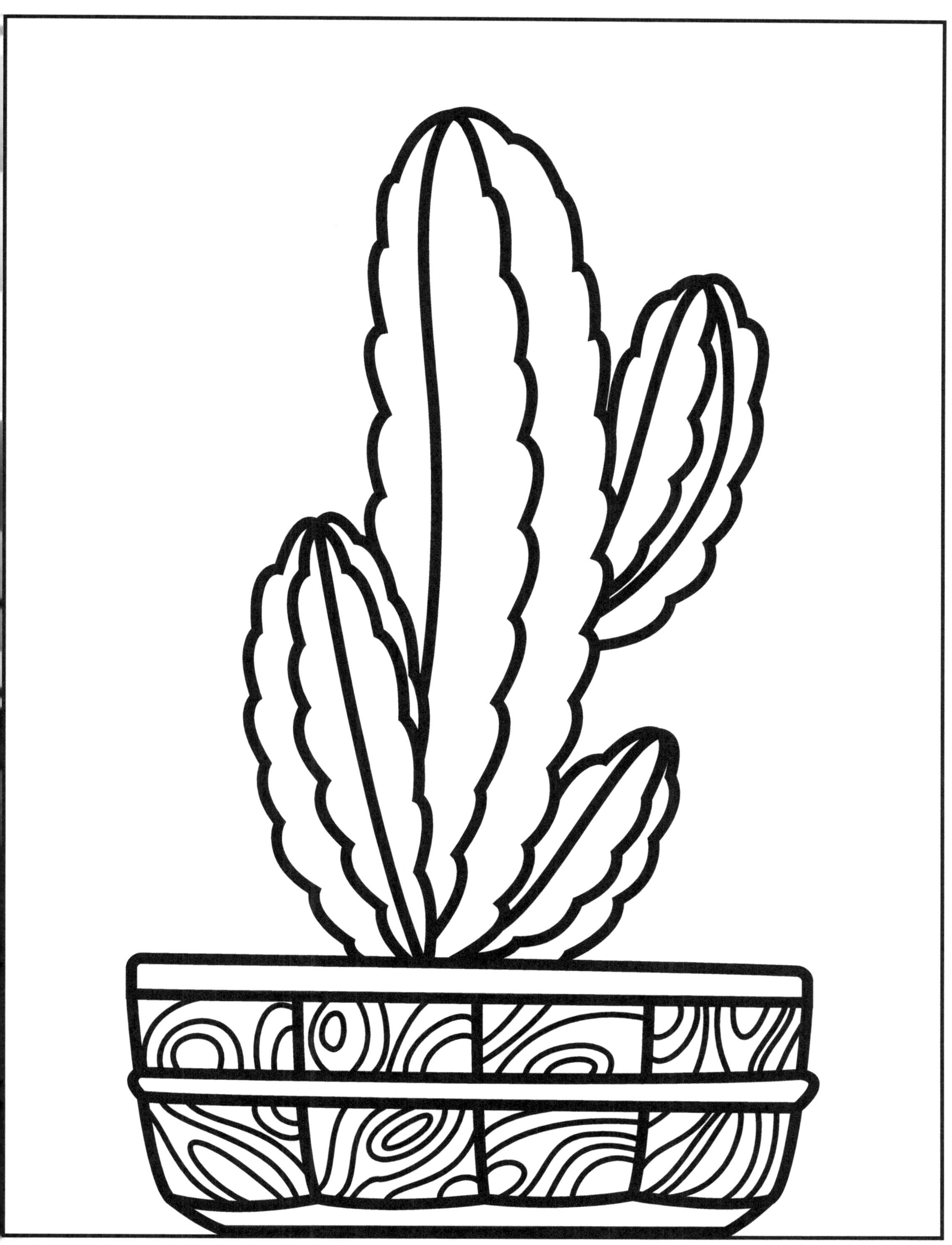

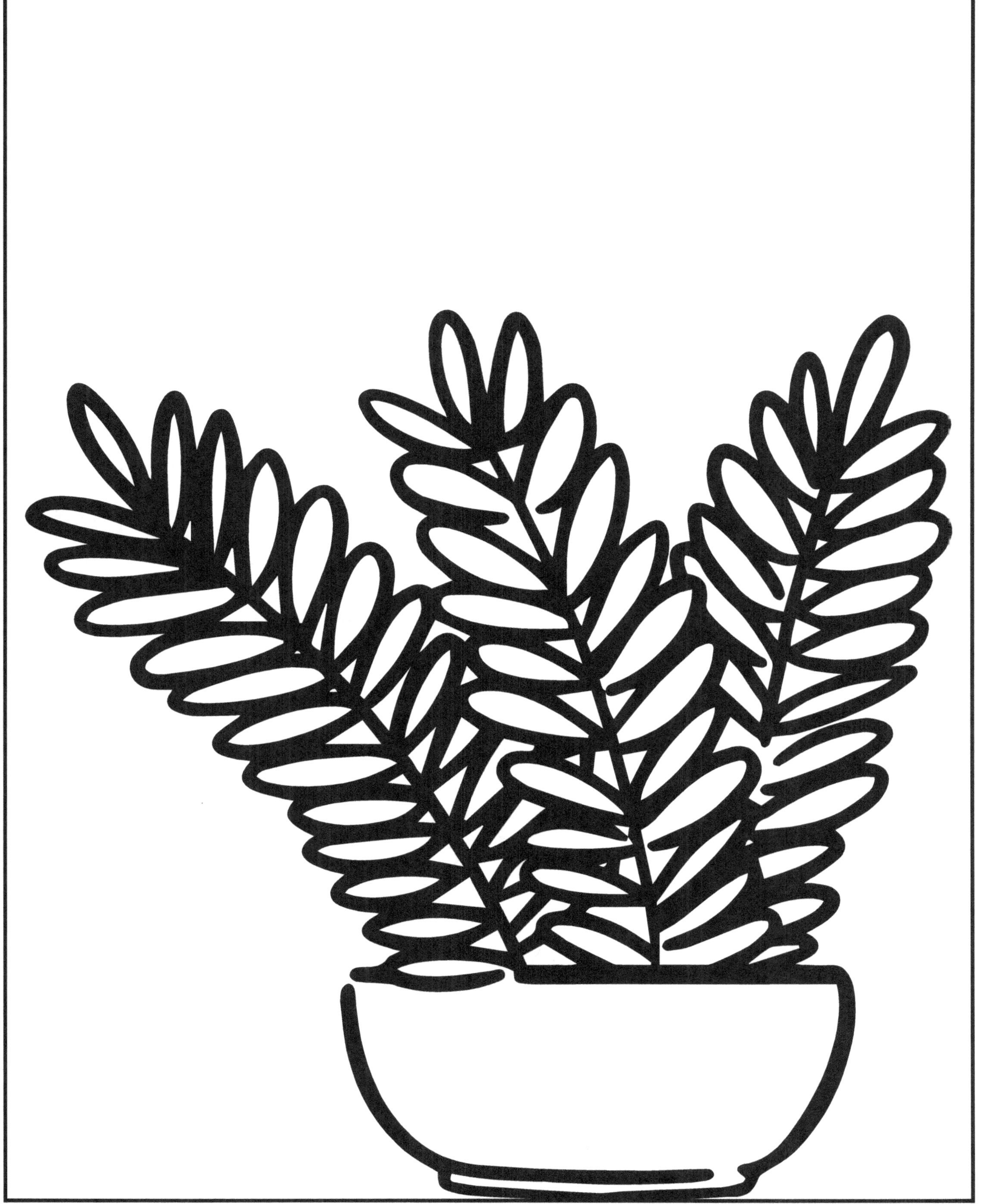

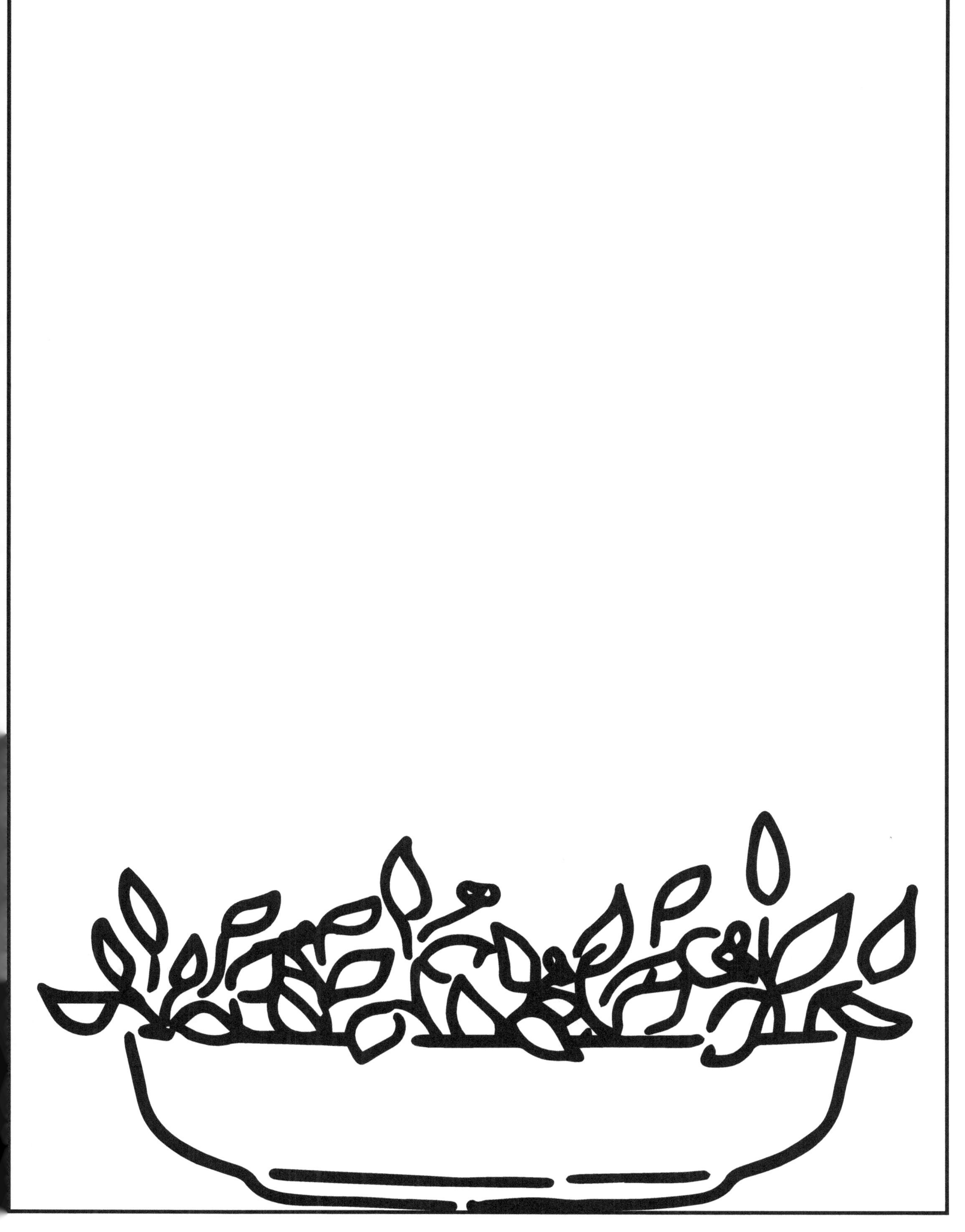

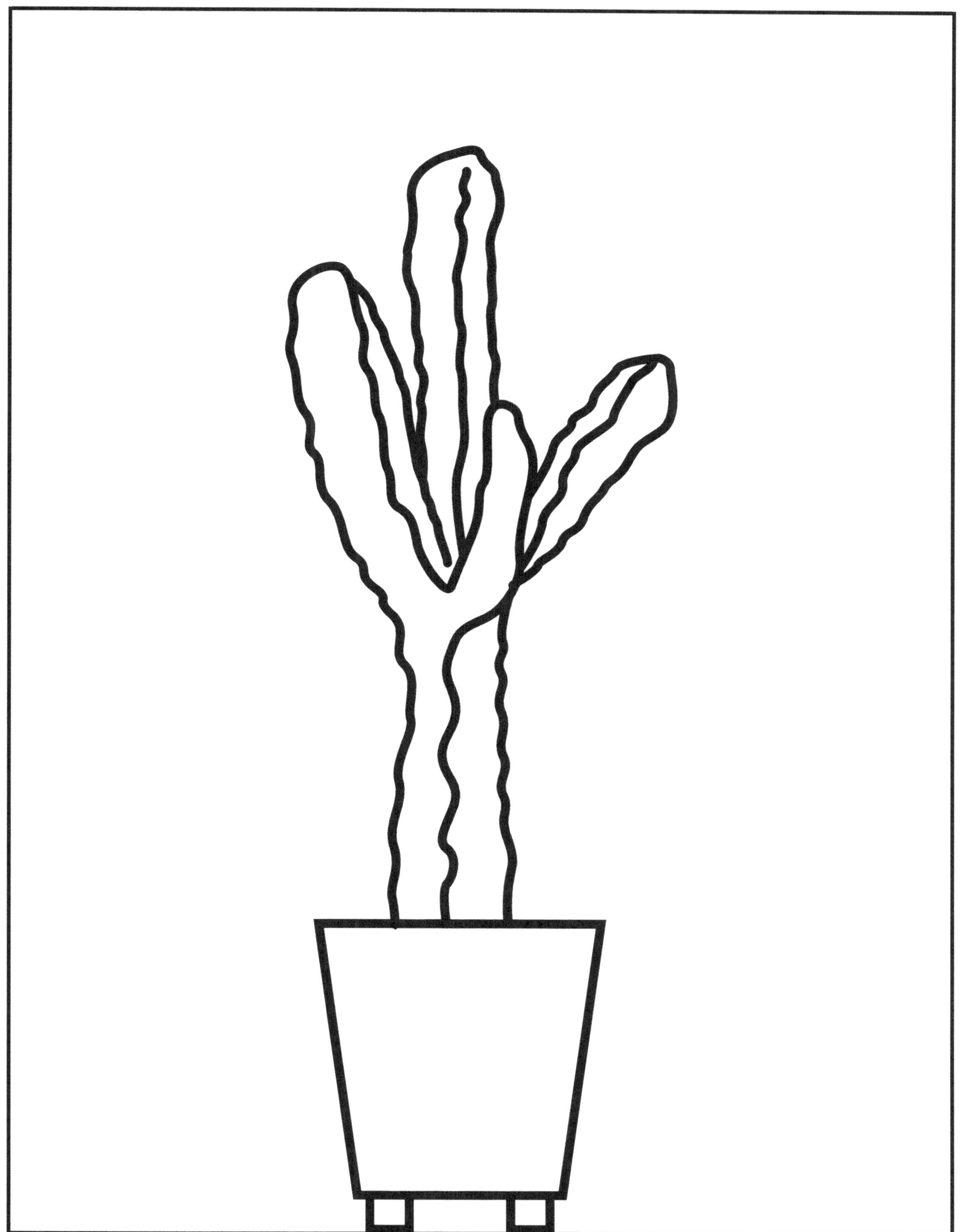

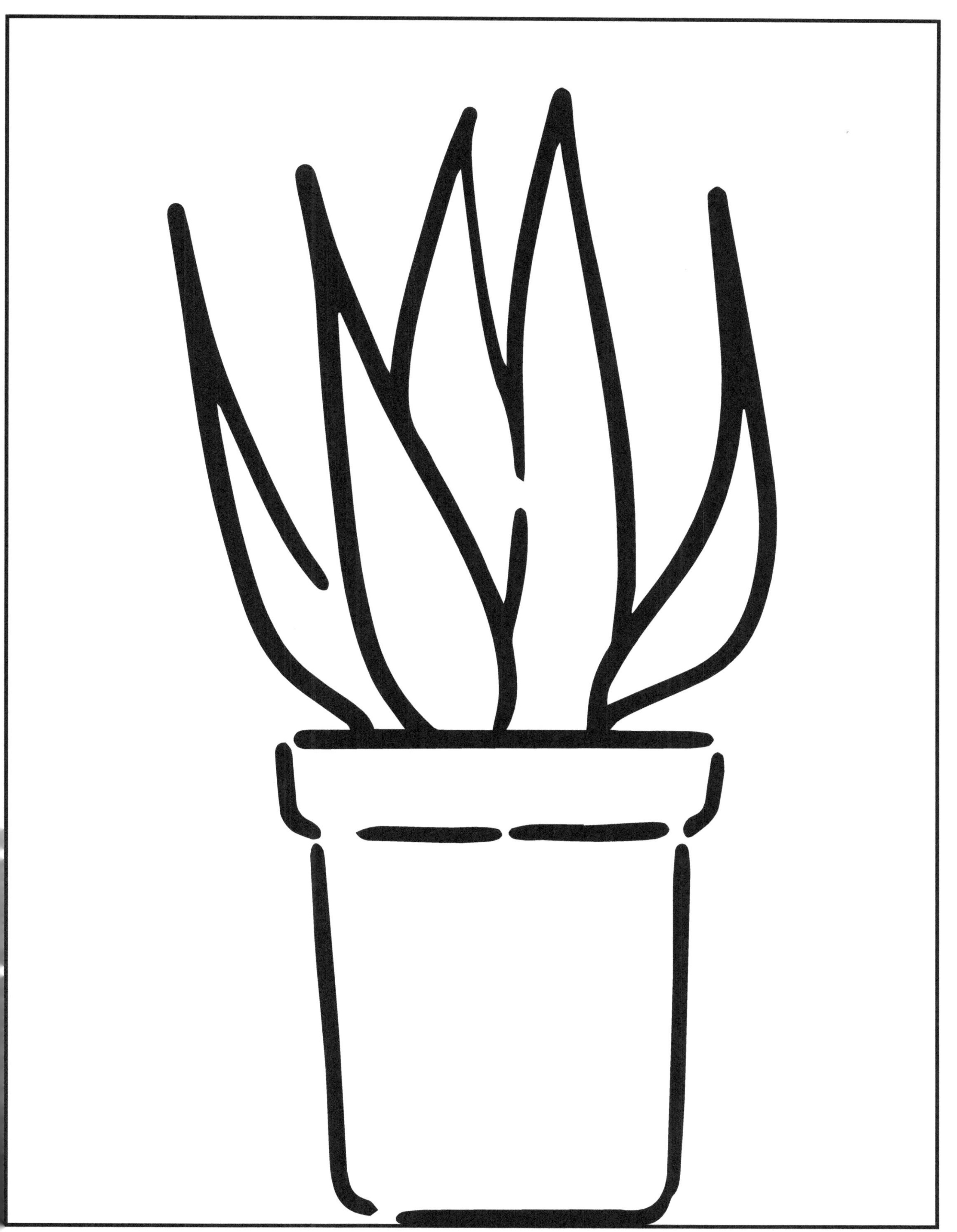

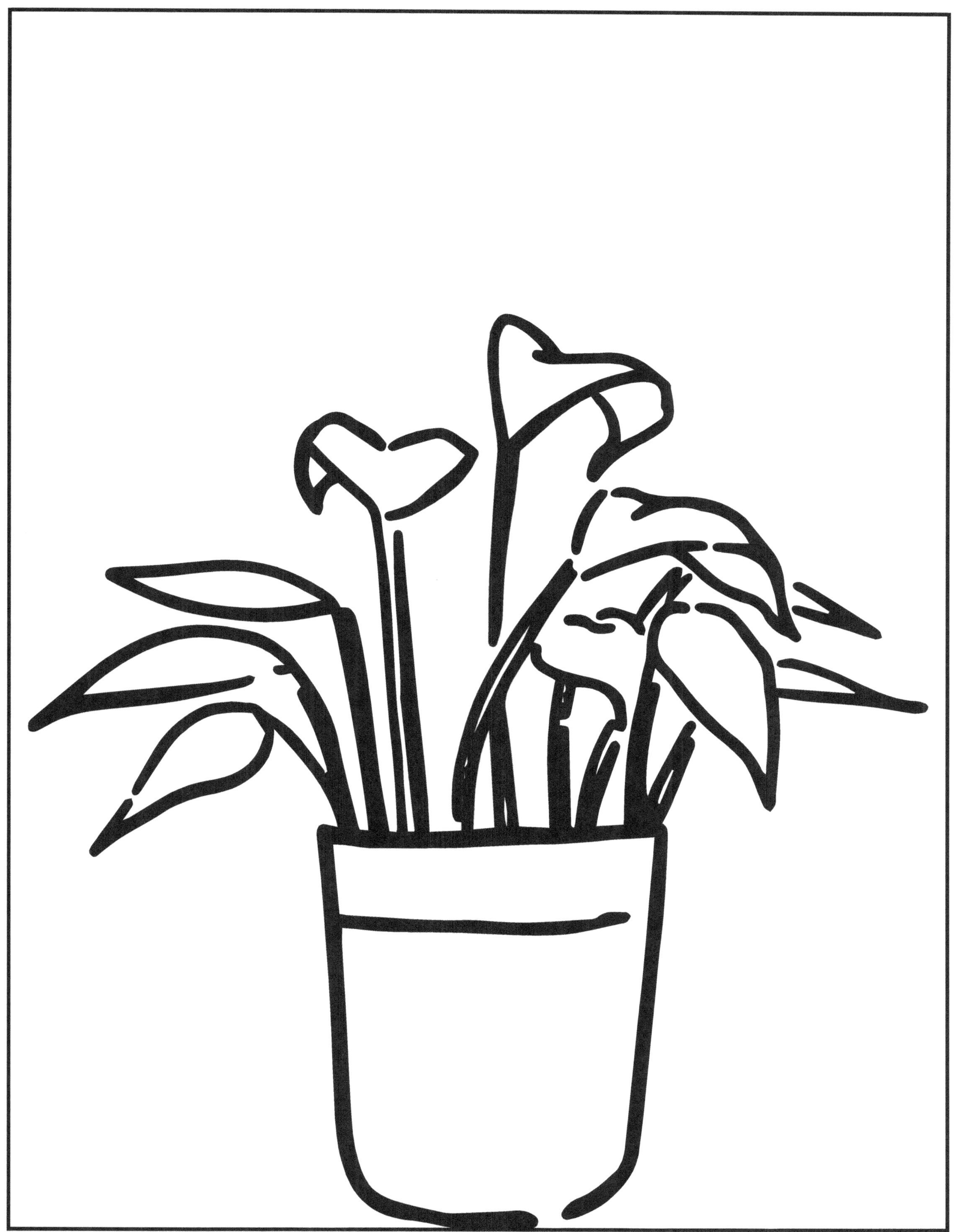

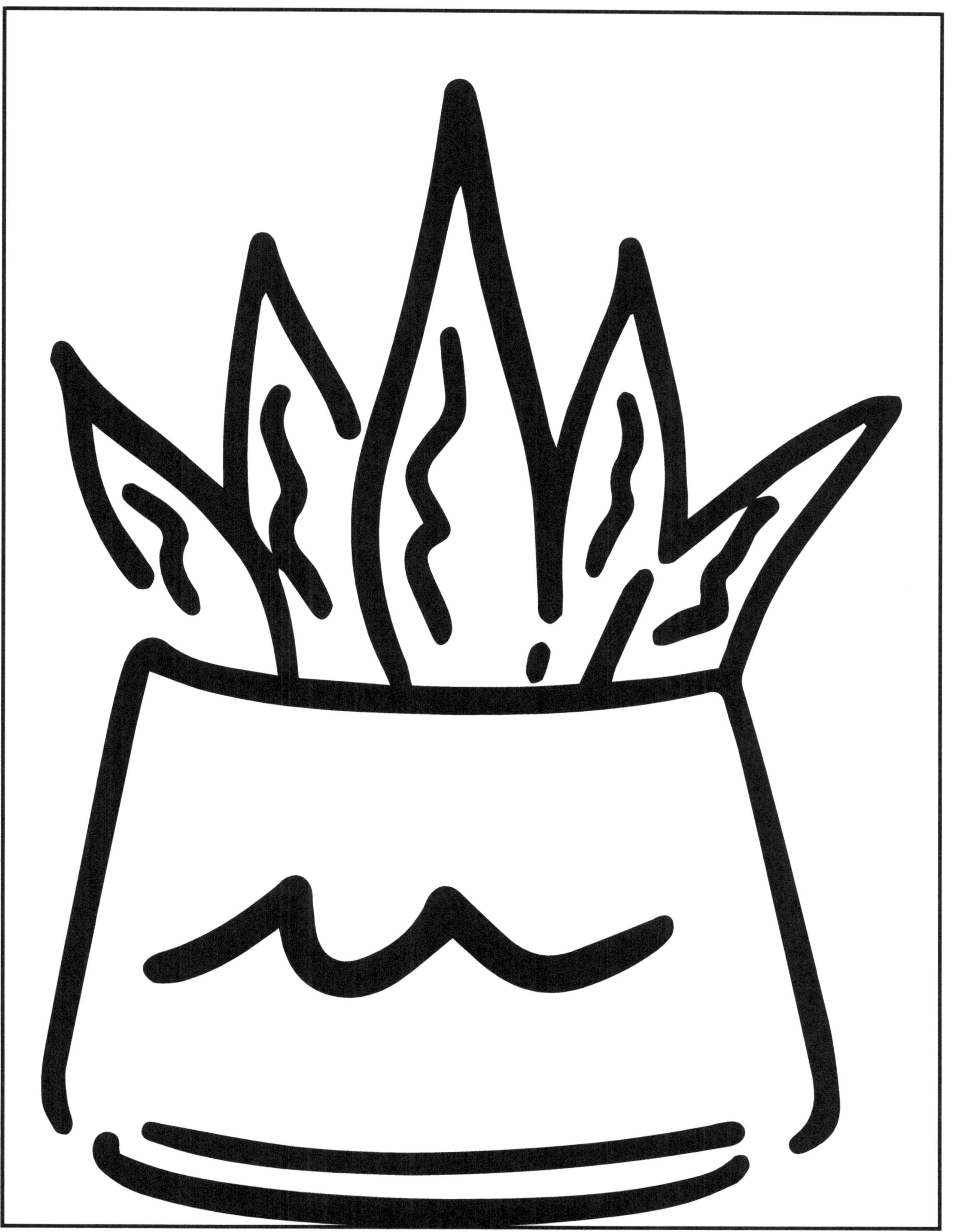

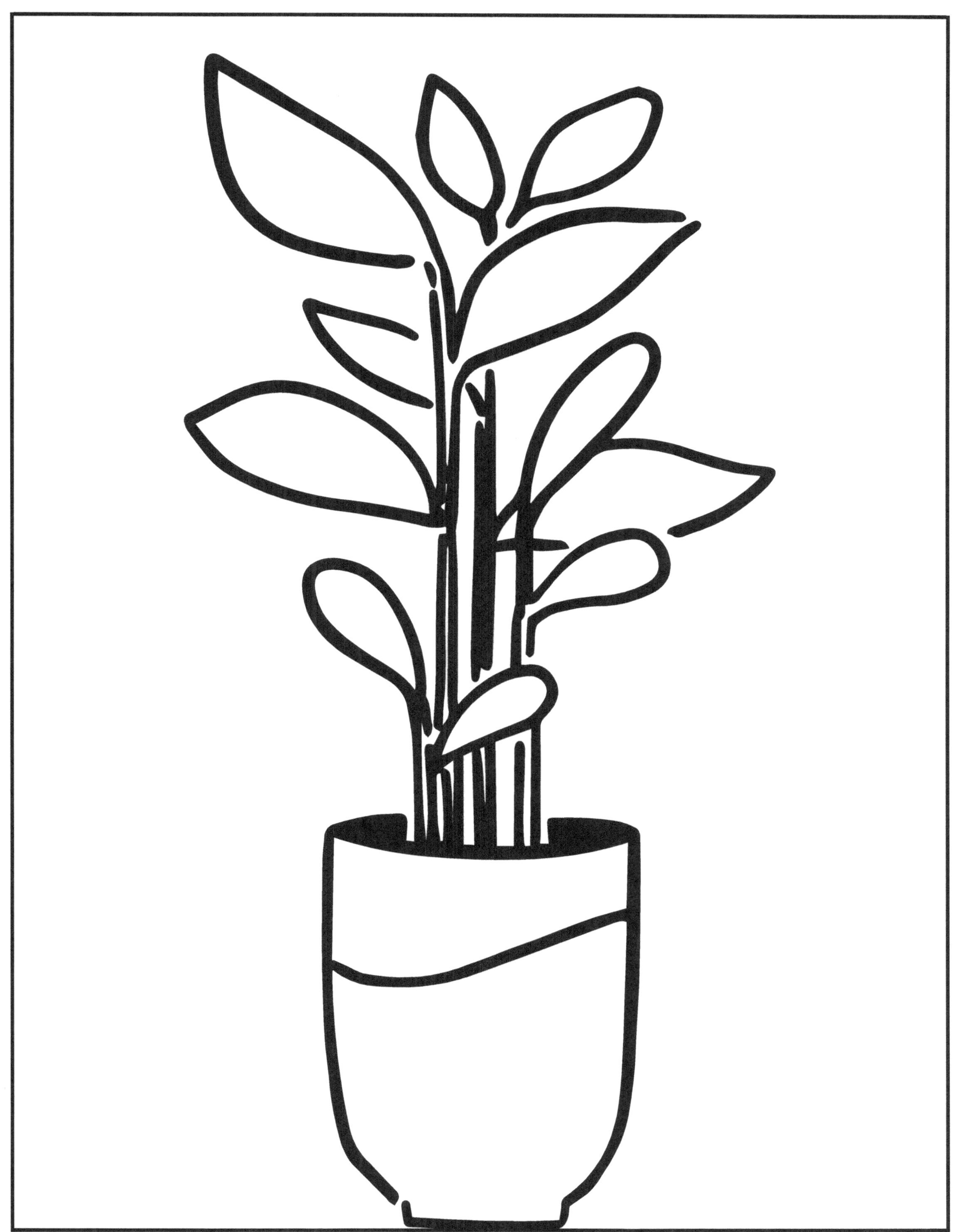

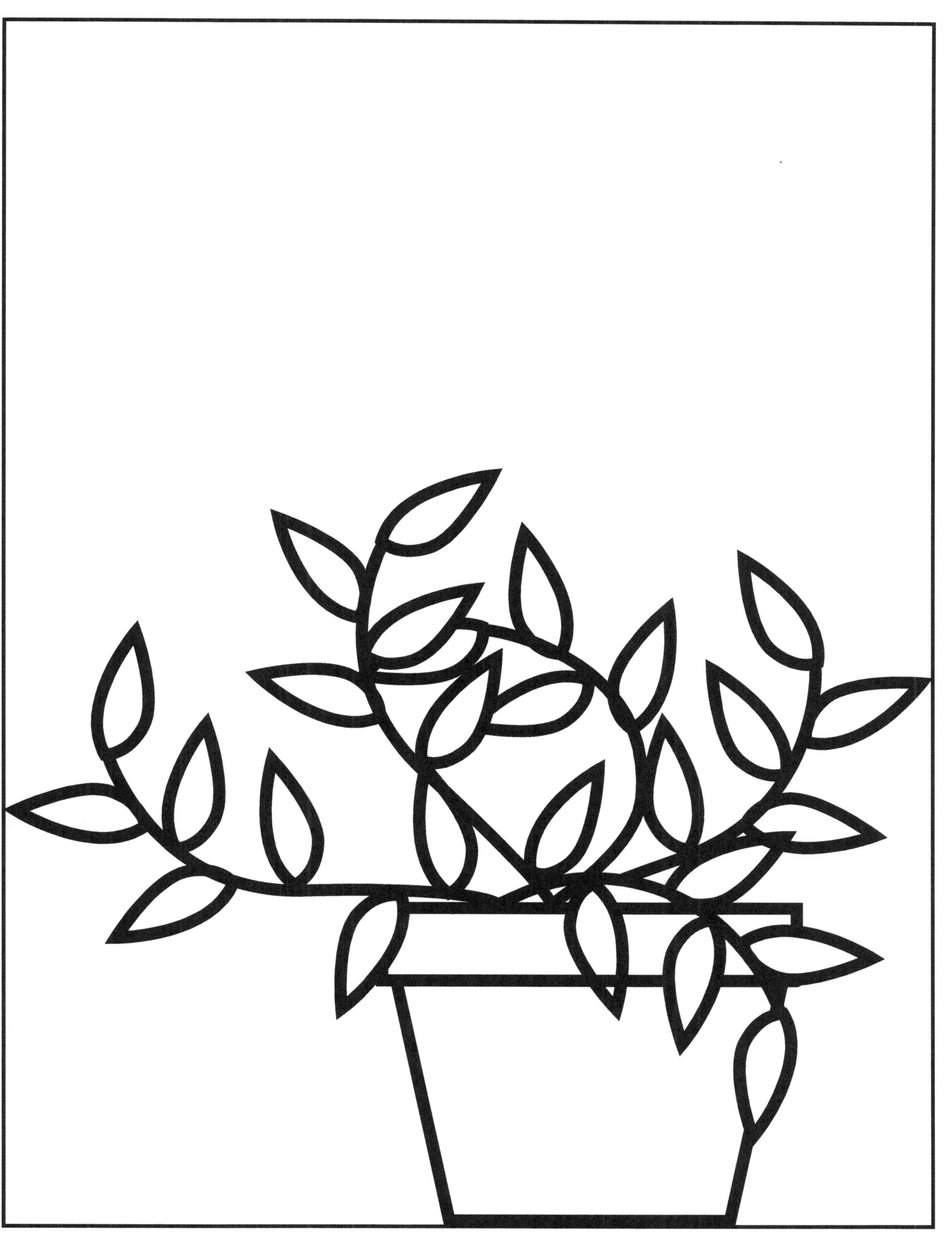

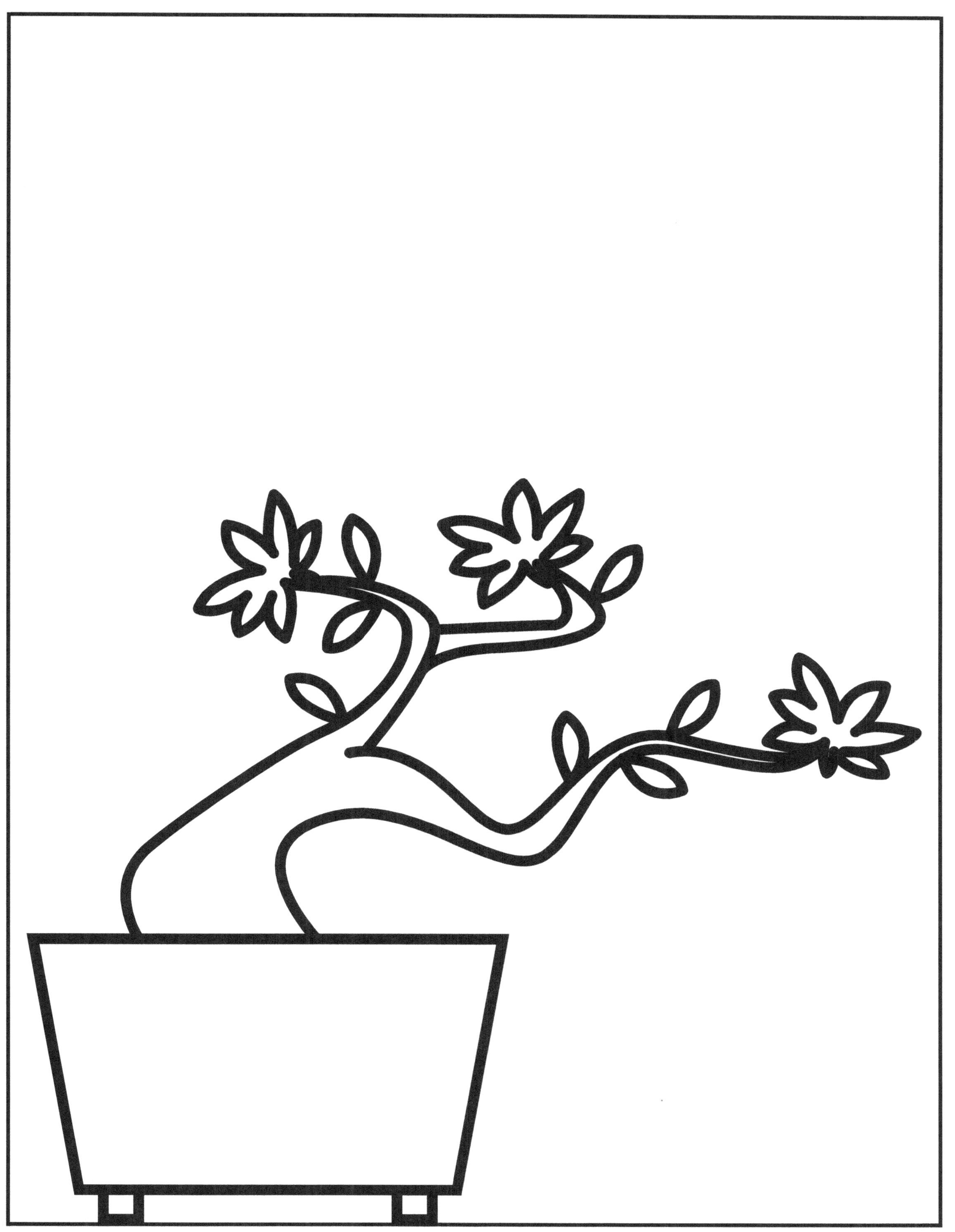

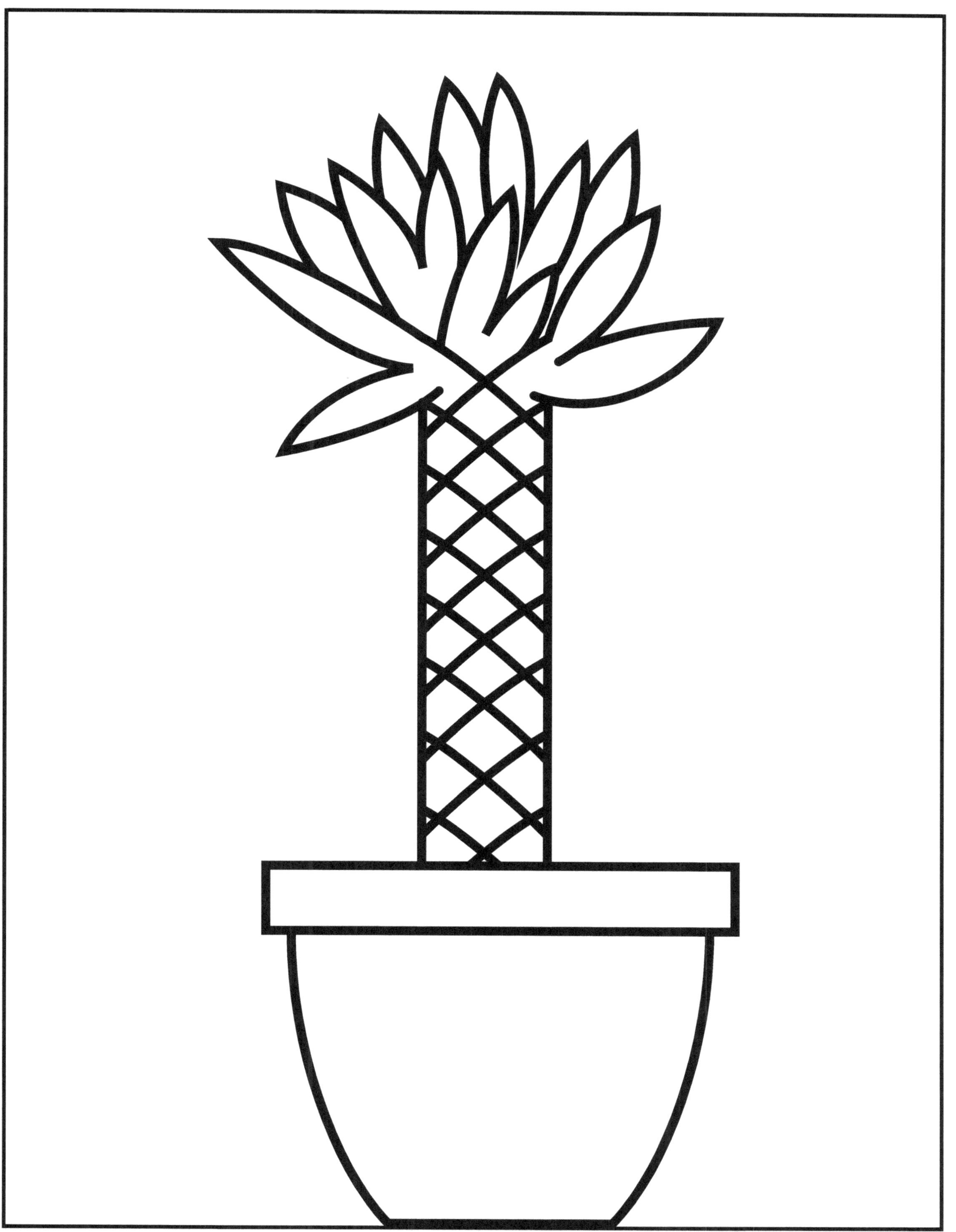

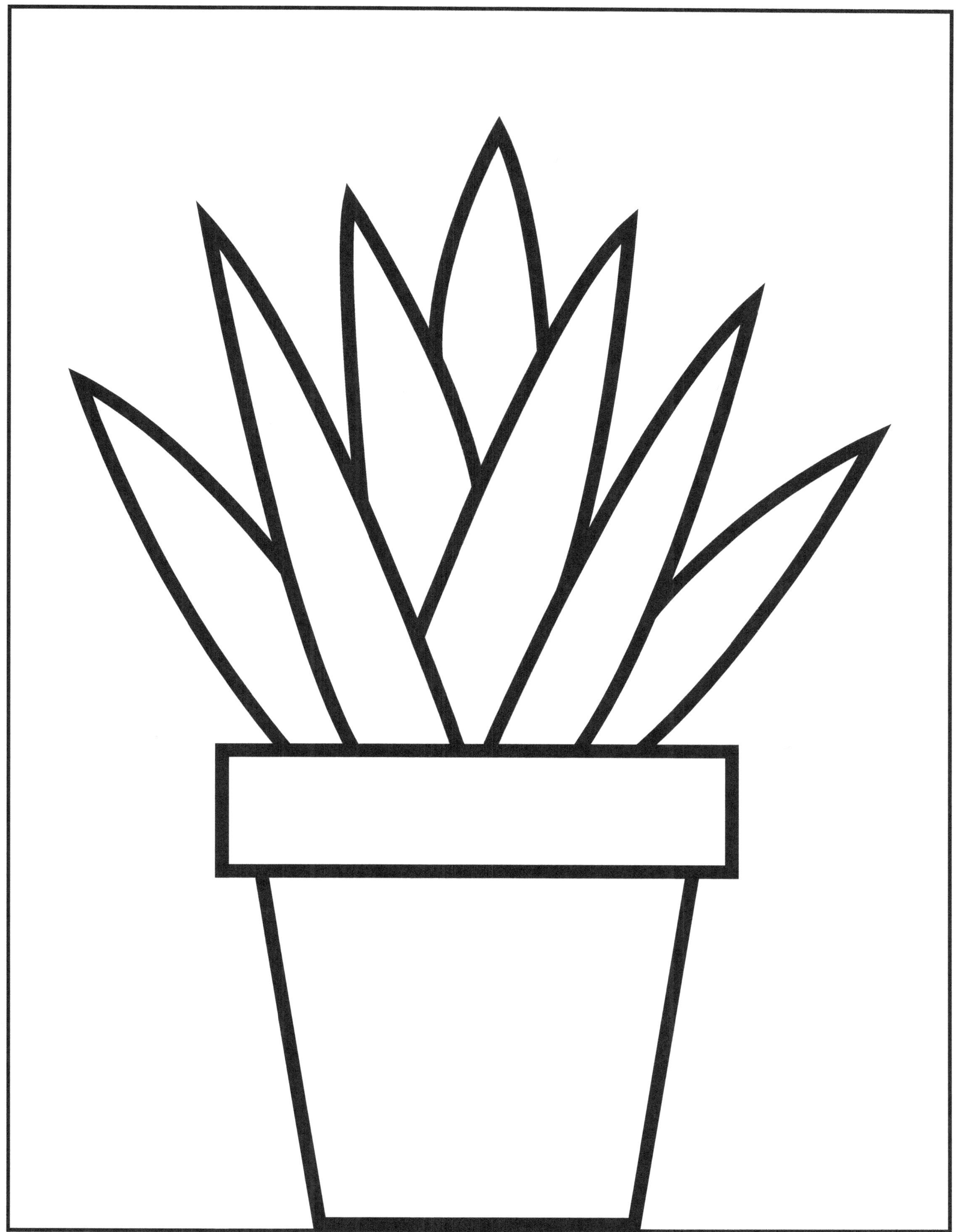

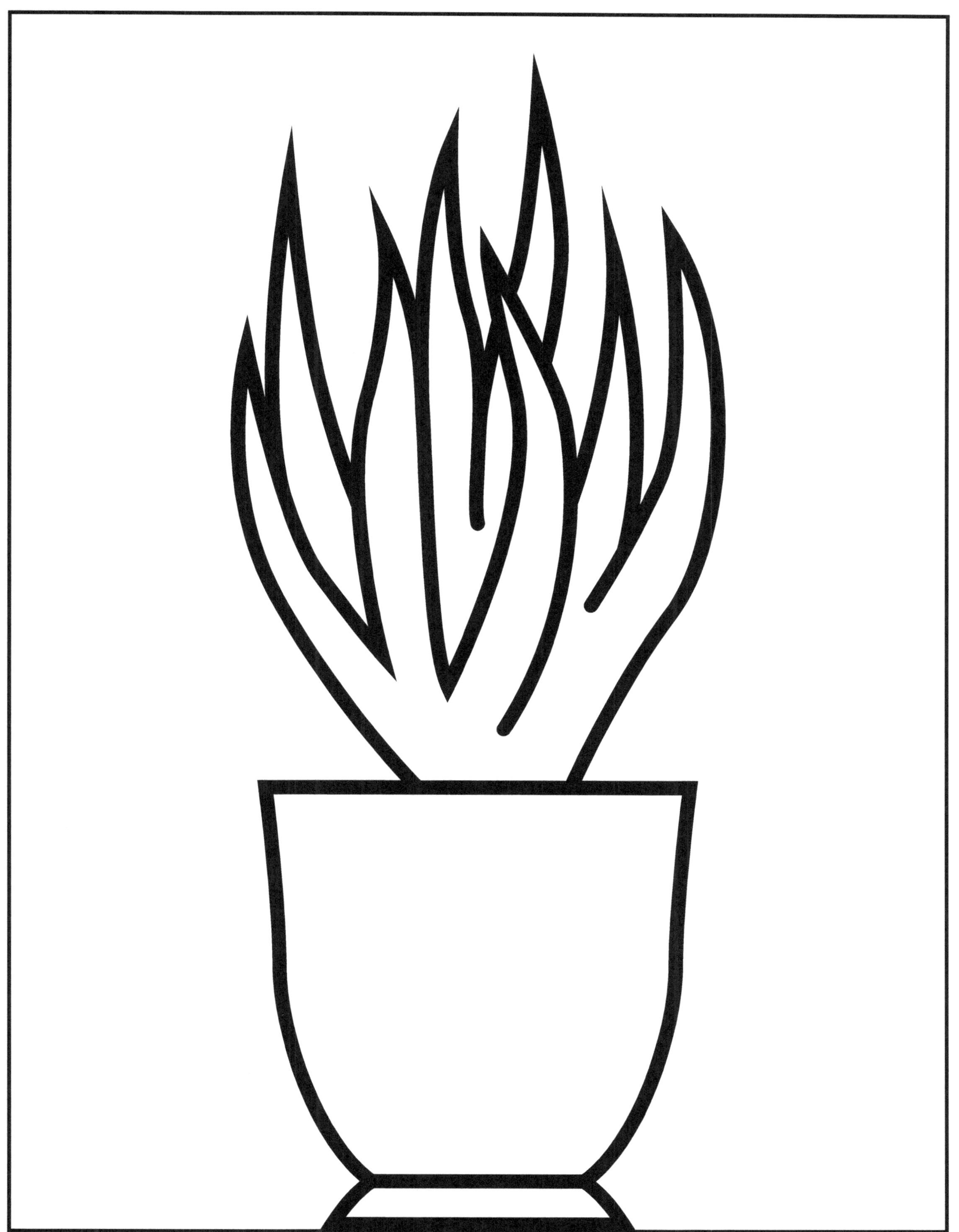